C-4428

MW01517563

THIS IS YOUR **PASSBOOK®** FOR ...

FISCAL SPECIALIST

NATIONAL LEARNING CORPORATION®

passbooks.com

PASSBOOK® SERIES

THE *PASSBOOK® SERIES* has been created to prepare applicants and candidates for the ultimate academic battlefield – the examination room.

At some time in our lives, each and every one of us may be required to take an examination – for validation, matriculation, admission, qualification, registration, certification, or licensure.

Based on the assumption that every applicant or candidate has met the basic formal educational standards, has taken the required number of courses, and read the necessary texts, the *PASSBOOK® SERIES* furnishes the one special preparation which may assure passing with confidence, instead of failing with insecurity. Examination questions – together with answers – are furnished as the basic vehicle for study so that the mysteries of the examination and its compounding difficulties may be eliminated or diminished by a sure method.

This book is meant to help you pass your examination provided that you qualify and are serious in your objective.

The entire field is reviewed through the huge store of content information which is succinctly presented through a provocative and challenging approach – the question-and-answer method.

A climate of success is established by furnishing the correct answers at the end of each test.

You soon learn to recognize types of questions, forms of questions, and patterns of questioning. You may even begin to anticipate expected outcomes.

You perceive that many questions are repeated or adapted so that you can gain acute insights, which may enable you to score many sure points.

You learn how to confront new questions, or types of questions, and to attack them confidently and work out the correct answers.

You note objectives and emphases, and recognize pitfalls and dangers, so that you may make positive educational adjustments.

Moreover, you are kept fully informed in relation to new concepts, methods, practices, and directions in the field.

You discover that you arre actually taking the examination all the time: you are preparing for the examination by "taking" an examination, not by reading extraneous and/or supererogatory textbooks.

In short, this PASSBOOK®, used directedly, should be an important factor in helping you to pass your test.

FISCAL SPECIALIST

DUTIES

Under general supervision perform one or more fiscal administrative support functions such as establishing and maintaining a comprehensive system for recording fiscal activity; coordinating expenditure control. Use established procedures in recording, summarizing and reporting fiscal activity.

TYPICAL WORK INCLUDES:

Review fiscal records, identify trends, and assist in formulating corrective actions;
Prepare, compile and provide fiscal reports such as year-end reports, budgetary reports, and auditing reports;
Receive electronic notices to establish accounts, set up new budget files and include the information in the appropriate databases;
Request Journal Vouchers for refund of incorrectly charged indirect costs, etc.;
Reverse expenditures (reimbursements to budgets);
Request corrections to charges made on our budgets in error;
Expenditure transfers between state budgets, grants and contracts;
Work to close expired/expiring budgets;
Fiscal planning, budget projection on grant budgets;
Request Advance budget numbers;
Set up sub-contracts with outside vendors;
Work to resolve errors in grant set-up and/or management issues.
Work with funding agencies and Principal Investigators (PIs) to resolve problems and/or obtain approval for deviation from authorized procedures or expenditures;
Reconcile all budgets on a monthly basis;
Prepare specialized reports to PIs;
Coordinate grant proposals with PIs to make sure everything is included and properly formatted;
Coordinate for timely review and submission of proposals;
Prepare budget revisions and other updates;
Perform related duties as required.

SAMPLE QUESTIONS

TEST 1

READING COMPREHENSION

DIRECTIONS: Read the following paragraphs. Your answers should be based only on the information contained in the paragraph. You may reread the paragraph as often as you wish. *PRINT THE LETTER OF THE CORRECT ANSWER IN THE SPACE AT THE RIGHT.*

Question 1.

DIRECTIONS: Question 1 should be answered on the basis of the following paragraph.

Often additional copies are needed of letters received. When this occurs, it will be necessary to make a notation on the back of the letters quoting the number of copies needed. Place all letters to be Xeroxed in the folders designated for this purpose. Place a rubber band around the folder and place it in the messenger bin. Usually letters are sent out once a day, depending on the quantity of papers received that day.

1. According to the above passage,   1._____
   A. a rubber band should be placed around all letters to be Xeroxed before placing them in the designated folder
   B. the number of copies needed of a letter should be noted on the front of the letter in the upper right-hand corner
   C. special folders are set aside in which to place letters that need to be Xeroxed
   D. generally, the messenger photocopies letters once a day, depending on the quantity of papers received that day

Question 2.

DIRECTIONS: Question 2 should be answered on the basis of the following paragraph.

To close out records of patients on the daily closure listing, follow these steps:

1. Pull patient's orange appointment card and chart.
2. Indicate "closed" on the chart and date closed.
3. Update the master card showing "closed" and date of closure write in red ink.
4. Destroy orange appointment card.
5. File chart and master card in closed files.

2. According to the above passage,   2.____
    A. when a patient's records are closed, his chart and master card are
       retained in closed files, but his appointment card is destroyed
    B. once "closed" and date of closure are properly shown on a patient's chart,
       master card and appointment card, the three documents should be filed in
       the closed files
    C. "closed" and date of closure should be written in red ink on the patient's
       master card and orange appointment card
    D. the orange appointment card should be destroyed after writing "closed"
       and date of closure on it

KEY (CORRECT ANSWERS)

1. C
2. A

TEST 2

PROGRESSION

DIRECTIONS: Each question or incomplete statement is followed by several suggested answers or completions. Select the one that BEST answers the question or completes the statement. *PRINT THE LETTER OF THE CORRECT ANSWER IN THE SPACE AT THE RIGHT.PRINT THE LETTER OF THE CORRECT ANSWER IN THE SPACE AT THE RIGHT.*

1. 5, 7, 10, 14, 19. The next number should be
   A. 24   B. 23   C. 25   D. 20

1.____

2. In this series, which number comes next: 7, 14, 28, 56, ?
   A. 112   B. 84   C. 42   D. 63

2.____

3. A, D, E, H, I. The next letters should be
   A. K   B. L   C. M   D. J

3.____

4. In this series, which letter comes next: C, B, A, F, E, D, I, H, ?
   A. K   B. J   C. G   D. L

4.____

KEY (CORRECT ANSWERS)

1. C
2. A
3. B
4. C

TEST 3

ARITHMETICAL COMPUTATIONS

DIRECTIONS: Perform the computation as indicated below and find the answer among the list of alternative responses. *PRINT THE LETTER OF THE CORRECT ANSWER IN THE SPACE AT THE RIGHT.*

1. $83 - 56 =$
    A. 23   B. 29   C. 33   D. 27   1.____

2. $15 + 17 =$
    A. 22   B. 32   C. 39   D. 42   2.____

3. $32 \times 7 =$
    A. 224   B. 234   C. 324   D. 334   3.____

4. $0.14 + 0.748 =$
    A. 8.88   B. 0.088   C. 0.788   D. 0.888   4.____

5. $50 + 49 =$
    A. 89   B. 90   C. 99   D. 109   5.____

6. $39 \times 2 =$
    A. 77   B. 78   C. 79   D. 81   6.____

KEY (CORRECT ANSWERS)

1.	D
2.	B
3.	A
4.	D
5.	C
6.	B

TEST 4

OFFICE PRACTICES AND PROCEDURES

DIRECTIONS: Each question or incomplete statement is followed by several suggested answers or completions. Select the one that BEST answers the question or completes the statement. *PRINT THE LETTER OF THE CORRECT ANSWER IN THE SPACE AT THE RIGHT.*

1. A pushbutton telephone with six buttons, one of which is a hold button, is often used when more than one outside line is needed.
   If you are talking on one line of this type of telephone when another call comes in, what is the procedure to follow if you were to answer the second call but keep the first call on the line?
   Push the
   A. hold button at the same time as you push the pickup button of the ringing line
   B. hold button and the push the pickup button of the ringing line
   C. pickup button of the ringing line and push the hold button
   D. pickup button of the ringing line and push the hold button when you return to the original line

   1.____

2. Suppose that you are asked to prepare a petty cash statement for March. The original and one copy are to go to the personnel office. One copy is to go to the fiscal office, and another copy is to go to your supervisor. The last copy is for your files.
   In preparing the statement and the copies, how many sheets of copy paper should you use?
   A. 4   B. 5   C. 6   D. 7

   2.____

3. Which of the following is the LEAST important advantage of putting the subject of a letter in the heading to the right of the address?
   A. Make filing of the copy easier
   B. Makes more space available in the body of the letter
   C. Simplified distribution of letters
   D. Simplifies determination of the subject of the letter

   3.____

KEY (CORRECT ANSWERS)

1. B
2. B
3. B

TEST 5

BOOKKEEPING PRINCIPLES, PRACTICES, AND PROCEDURES

DIRECTIONS: Each question or incomplete statement is followed by several suggested answers or completions. Select the one that BEST answers the question or completes the statement. *PRINT THE LETTER OF THE CORRECT ANSWER IN THE SPACE AT THE RIGHT.*

1. A credit to a revenue account   1.____
    A. decreases revenues   B. increases equity
    C. decreases equity   D. increases assets

2. Funds that have been consumed in producing revenue are referred to as   2.____
    A. losses   B. charges   C. liabilities   D. expenses

3. An amount, payable in money, goods, or services, owed by a business to a   3.____
    creditor is known as a(n)
    A. equity   B. debt   C. liability   D. asset

4. The inventory valuation system which assumes that merchandise is sold in   4.____
    the order in which the purchase expenditures were made is called the _____
    system.
    A. perpetual inventory   B. first-in, first-out (FIFO)
    C. periodic inventory   D. weighted average
    E. last-in, first-out (LIFO)

5. The "Straight-Line" method of depreciation assumes that the   5.____
    A. amount charged to operation, if placed on interest, will accumulate to
       more than the amount to be depreciated
    B. asset being depreciated will usually require heavier rep in the later
       periods
    C. rate of return of an asset depreciated decreases with the age of the asset
    D. depreciation of an asset is a uniform function of time

KEY (CORRECT ANSWERS)

1.	B
2.	D
3.	C
4.	B
5.	D

TEST 6

TRANSACTIONS – DEBITS & CREDITS

DIRECTIONS: The following questions are based on transactions which occurred during the current accounting period. In answering these questions, you should choose the correct journal entry for the transaction listed. Use only the following listed accounts in formulating your journal entry. *PRINT THE LETTER OF THE CORRECT ANSWER IN THE SPACE AT THE RIGHT.*

Rook, Incorporated is a major department store in this area. Below is a partial list of accounts used in the business.

Accounts Payable	Interest Receivable
Accounts Receivable	Notes Payable
Allowance for Bad Debts	Prepaid Taxes
Bad Debts Expense	Purchases
Cash	Purchase Returns & Allowances
Cash Dividends	Retained Earnings
Common Stock	Sales
Insurance Expense	Sales Returns & Allowances
Interest Expense	Taxes Payable
Interest Income	Tax Expense

1.   The company bought merchandise totaling $500 on account: 1._____
    A. debit Accounts Payable; credit Cash
    B. debit Purchases; credit Accounts Payable
    C. debit Cash; credit Sales
    D. debit Accounts Payable; credit Purchases
    E. debit Purchases; credit Cash

2.   A customer returned merchandise that he had previously purchased on   2._____
    account:
    A. debit Sales Returns and Allowances; credit Accounts Receivable
    B. debit Sales Returns and Allowances; credit Cash
    C. debit Cash; credit Accounts Receivable
    D. debit Sales Returns and Allowances; credit Accounts Receivable, Sales

3.   Received payment from a customer on account; the payment included interest   3._____
    charges:
    A. debit Interest Income; credit Cash
    B. debit Notes Payable, Cash; credit Interest Income, Accounts Receivable
    C. debit Cash; credit Accounts Receivable
    D. debit Accounts Receivable; credit Cash, Interest Income
    E. debit Cash; credit Accounts Receivable, Interest Income

KEY (CORRECT ANSWERS)

1.   B
2.   A
3.   E

_____

HOW TO TAKE A TEST

I. YOU MUST PASS AN EXAMINATION

A. WHAT EVERY CANDIDATE SHOULD KNOW

Examination applicants often ask us for help in preparing for the written test. What can I study in advance? What kinds of questions will be asked? How will the test be given? How will the papers be graded?

As an applicant for a civil service examination, you may be wondering about some of these things. Our purpose here is to suggest effective methods of advance study and to describe civil service examinations.

Your chances for success on this examination can be increased if you know how to prepare. Those "pre-examination jitters" can be reduced if you know what to expect. You can even experience an adventure in good citizenship if you know why civil service exams are given.

B. WHY ARE CIVIL SERVICE EXAMINATIONS GIVEN?

Civil service examinations are important to you in two ways. As a citizen, you want public jobs filled by employees who know how to do their work. As a job seeker, you want a fair chance to compete for that job on an equal footing with other candidates. The best-known means of accomplishing this two-fold goal is the competitive examination.

Exams are widely publicized throughout the nation. They may be administered for jobs in federal, state, city, municipal, town or village governments or agencies.

Any citizen may apply, with some limitations, such as the age or residence of applicants. Your experience and education may be reviewed to see whether you meet the requirements for the particular examination. When these requirements exist, they are reasonable and applied consistently to all applicants. Thus, a competitive examination may cause you some uneasiness now, but it is your privilege and safeguard.

C. HOW ARE CIVIL SERVICE EXAMS DEVELOPED?

Examinations are carefully written by trained technicians who are specialists in the field known as "psychological measurement," in consultation with recognized authorities in the field of work that the test will cover. These experts recommend the subject matter areas or skills to be tested; only those knowledges or skills important to your success on the job are included. The most reliable books and source materials available are used as references. Together, the experts and technicians judge the difficulty level of the questions.

Test technicians know how to phrase questions so that the problem is clearly stated. Their ethics do not permit "trick" or "catch" questions. Questions may have been tried out on sample groups, or subjected to statistical analysis, to determine their usefulness.

Written tests are often used in combination with performance tests, ratings of training and experience, and oral interviews. All of these measures combine to form the best-known means of finding the right person for the right job.

II. HOW TO PASS THE WRITTEN TEST

A. NATURE OF THE EXAMINATION

To prepare intelligently for civil service examinations, you should know how they differ from school examinations you have taken. In school you were assigned certain definite pages to read or subjects to cover. The examination questions were quite detailed and usually emphasized memory. Civil service exams, on the other hand, try to discover your present ability to perform the duties of a position, plus your potentiality to learn these duties. In other words, a civil service exam attempts to predict how successful you will be. Questions cover such a broad area that they cannot be as minute and detailed as school exam questions.

In the public service similar kinds of work, or positions, are grouped together in one "class." This process is known as *position-classification*. All the positions in a class are paid according to the salary range for that class. One class title covers all of these positions, and they are all tested by the same examination.

B. FOUR BASIC STEPS

1) Study the announcement

How, then, can you know what subjects to study? Our best answer is: "Learn as much as possible about the class of positions for which you've applied." The exam will test the knowledge, skills and abilities needed to do the work.

Your most valuable source of information about the position you want is the official exam announcement. This announcement lists the training and experience qualifications. Check these standards and apply only if you come reasonably close to meeting them.

The brief description of the position in the examination announcement offers some clues to the subjects which will be tested. Think about the job itself. Review the duties in your mind. Can you perform them, or are there some in which you are rusty? Fill in the blank spots in your preparation.

Many jurisdictions preview the written test in the exam announcement by including a section called "Knowledge and Abilities Required," "Scope of the Examination," or some similar heading. Here you will find out specifically what fields will be tested.

2) Review your own background

Once you learn in general what the position is all about, and what you need to know to do the work, ask yourself which subjects you already know fairly well and which need improvement. You may wonder whether to concentrate on improving your strong areas or on building some background in your fields of weakness. When the announcement has specified "some knowledge" or "considerable knowledge," or has used adjectives like "beginning principles of…" or "advanced … methods," you can get a clue as to the number and difficulty of questions to be asked in any given field. More questions, and hence broader coverage, would be included for those subjects which are more important in the work. Now weigh your strengths and weaknesses against the job requirements and prepare accordingly.

3) Determine the level of the position

Another way to tell how intensively you should prepare is to understand the level of the job for which you are applying. Is it the entering level? In other words, is this the position in which beginners in a field of work are hired? Or is it an intermediate or advanced level? Sometimes this is indicated by such words as "Junior" or "Senior" in the class title. Other jurisdictions use Roman numerals to designate the level – Clerk I, Clerk II, for example. The word "Supervisor" sometimes appears in the title. If the level is not indicated by the title, check the description of duties. Will you be working under very close supervision, or will you have responsibility for independent decisions in this work?

4) Choose appropriate study materials

Now that you know the subjects to be examined and the relative amount of each subject to be covered, you can choose suitable study materials. For beginning level jobs, or even advanced ones, if you have a pronounced weakness in some aspect of your training, read a modern, standard textbook in that field. Be sure it is up to date and has general coverage. Such books are normally available at your library, and the librarian will be glad to help you locate one. For entry-level positions, questions of appropriate difficulty are chosen – neither highly advanced questions, nor those too simple. Such questions require careful thought but not advanced training.

If the position for which you are applying is technical or advanced, you will read more advanced, specialized material. If you are already familiar with the basic principles of your field, elementary textbooks would waste your time. Concentrate on advanced textbooks and technical periodicals. Think through the concepts and review difficult problems in your field.

These are all general sources. You can get more ideas on your own initiative, following these leads. For example, training manuals and publications of the government agency which employs workers in your field can be useful, particularly for technical and professional positions. A letter or visit to the government department involved may result in more specific study suggestions, and certainly will provide you with a more definite idea of the exact nature of the position you are seeking.

III. KINDS OF TESTS

Tests are used for purposes other than measuring knowledge and ability to perform specified duties. For some positions, it is equally important to test ability to make adjustments to new situations or to profit from training. In others, basic mental abilities not dependent on information are essential. Questions which test these things may not appear as pertinent to the duties of the position as those which test for knowledge and information. Yet they are often highly important parts of a fair examination. For very general questions, it is almost impossible to help you direct your study efforts. What we can do is to point out some of the more common of these general abilities needed in public service positions and describe some typical questions.

1) General information

Broad, general information has been found useful for predicting job success in some kinds of work. This is tested in a variety of ways, from vocabulary lists to questions about current events. Basic background in some field of work, such as sociology or economics, may be sampled in a group of questions. Often these are principles which have become familiar to most persons through exposure rather than through formal training. It is difficult to advise you how to study for these questions; being alert to the world around you is our best suggestion.

2) Verbal ability

An example of an ability needed in many positions is verbal or language ability. Verbal ability is, in brief, the ability to use and understand words. Vocabulary and grammar tests are typical measures of this ability. Reading comprehension or paragraph interpretation questions are common in many kinds of civil service tests. You are given a paragraph of written material and asked to find its central meaning.

3) Numerical ability

Number skills can be tested by the familiar arithmetic problem, by checking paired lists of numbers to see which are alike and which are different, or by interpreting charts and graphs. In the latter test, a graph may be printed in the test booklet which you are asked to use as the basis for answering questions.

4) Observation

A popular test for law-enforcement positions is the observation test. A picture is shown to you for several minutes, then taken away. Questions about the picture test your ability to observe both details and larger elements.

5) Following directions

In many positions in the public service, the employee must be able to carry out written instructions dependably and accurately. You may be given a chart with several columns, each column listing a variety of information. The questions require you to carry out directions involving the information given in the chart.

6) Skills and aptitudes

Performance tests effectively measure some manual skills and aptitudes. When the skill is one in which you are trained, such as typing or shorthand, you can practice. These tests are often very much like those given in business school or high school courses. For many of the other skills and aptitudes, however, no short-time preparation can be made. Skills and abilities natural to you or that you have developed throughout your lifetime are being tested.

Many of the general questions just described provide all the data needed to answer the questions and ask you to use your reasoning ability to find the answers. Your best preparation for these tests, as well as for tests of facts and ideas, is to be at your physical and mental best. You, no doubt, have your own methods of getting into an exam-taking mood and keeping "in shape." The next section lists some ideas on this subject.

IV. KINDS OF QUESTIONS

Only rarely is the "essay" question, which you answer in narrative form, used in civil service tests. Civil service tests are usually of the short-answer type. Full instructions for answering these questions will be given to you at the examination. But in case this is your first experience with short-answer questions and separate answer sheets, here is what you need to know:

1) Multiple-choice Questions

Most popular of the short-answer questions is the "multiple choice" or "best answer" question. It can be used, for example, to test for factual knowledge, ability to solve problems or judgment in meeting situations found at work.

A multiple-choice question is normally one of three types—

- It can begin with an incomplete statement followed by several possible endings. You are to find the one ending which *best* completes the statement, although some of the others may not be entirely wrong.
- It can also be a complete statement in the form of a question which is answered by choosing one of the statements listed.
- It can be in the form of a problem – again you select the best answer.

Here is an example of a multiple-choice question with a discussion which should give you some clues as to the method for choosing the right answer:

When an employee has a complaint about his assignment, the action which will *best* help him overcome his difficulty is to
- A. discuss his difficulty with his coworkers
- B. take the problem to the head of the organization
- C. take the problem to the person who gave him the assignment
- D. say nothing to anyone about his complaint

In answering this question, you should study each of the choices to find which is best. Consider choice "A" – Certainly an employee may discuss his complaint with fellow employees, but no change or improvement can result, and the complaint remains unresolved. Choice "B" is a poor choice since the head of the organization probably does not know what assignment you have been given, and taking your problem to him is known as "going over the head" of the supervisor. The supervisor, or person who made the assignment, is the person who can clarify it or correct any injustice. Choice "C" is, therefore, correct. To say nothing, as in choice "D," is unwise. Supervisors have and interest in knowing the problems employees are facing, and the employee is seeking a solution to his problem.

2) True/False Questions

The "true/false" or "right/wrong" form of question is sometimes used. Here a complete statement is given. Your job is to decide whether the statement is right or wrong.

SAMPLE: A roaming cell-phone call to a nearby city costs less than a non-roaming call to a distant city.

This statement is wrong, or false, since roaming calls are more expensive.
This is not a complete list of all possible question forms, although most of the others are variations of these common types. You will always get complete directions for

answering questions. Be sure you understand *how* to mark your answers – ask questions until you do.

V. RECORDING YOUR ANSWERS

Computer terminals are used more and more today for many different kinds of exams.

For an examination with very few applicants, you may be told to record your answers in the test booklet itself. Separate answer sheets are much more common. If this separate answer sheet is to be scored by machine – and this is often the case – it is highly important that you mark your answers correctly in order to get credit.

An electronic scoring machine is often used in civil service offices because of the speed with which papers can be scored. Machine-scored answer sheets must be marked with a pencil, which will be given to you. This pencil has a high graphite content which responds to the electronic scoring machine. As a matter of fact, stray dots may register as answers, so do not let your pencil rest on the answer sheet while you are pondering the correct answer. Also, if your pencil lead breaks or is otherwise defective, ask for another.

Since the answer sheet will be dropped in a slot in the scoring machine, be careful not to bend the corners or get the paper crumpled.

The answer sheet normally has five vertical columns of numbers, with 30 numbers to a column. These numbers correspond to the question numbers in your test booklet. After each number, going across the page are four or five pairs of dotted lines. These short dotted lines have small letters or numbers above them. The first two pairs may also have a "T" or "F" above the letters. This indicates that the first two pairs only are to be used if the questions are of the true-false type. If the questions are multiple choice, disregard the "T" and "F" and pay attention only to the small letters or numbers.

Answer your questions in the manner of the sample that follows:

32. The largest city in the United States is
A. Washington, D.C.
B. New York City
C. Chicago
D. Detroit
E. San Francisco

1) Choose the answer you think is best. (New York City is the largest, so "B" is correct.)
2) Find the row of dotted lines numbered the same as the question you are answering. (Find row number 32)
3) Find the pair of dotted lines corresponding to the answer. (Find the pair of lines under the mark "B.")
4) Make a solid black mark between the dotted lines.

VI. BEFORE THE TEST

Common sense will help you find procedures to follow to get ready for an examination. Too many of us, however, overlook these sensible measures. Indeed, nervousness and fatigue have been found to be the most serious reasons why applicants fail to do their best on civil service tests. Here is a list of reminders:

- Begin your preparation early – Don't wait until the last minute to go scurrying around for books and materials or to find out what the position is all about.
- Prepare continuously – An hour a night for a week is better than an all-night cram session. This has been definitely established. What is more, a night a week for a month will return better dividends than crowding your study into a shorter period of time.
- Locate the place of the exam – You have been sent a notice telling you when and where to report for the examination. If the location is in a different town or otherwise unfamiliar to you, it would be well to inquire the best route and learn something about the building.
- Relax the night before the test – Allow your mind to rest. Do not study at all that night. Plan some mild recreation or diversion; then go to bed early and get a good night's sleep.
- Get up early enough to make a leisurely trip to the place for the test – This way unforeseen events, traffic snarls, unfamiliar buildings, etc. will not upset you.
- Dress comfortably – A written test is not a fashion show. You will be known by number and not by name, so wear something comfortable.
- Leave excess paraphernalia at home – Shopping bags and odd bundles will get in your way. You need bring only the items mentioned in the official notice you received; usually everything you need is provided. Do not bring reference books to the exam. They will only confuse those last minutes and be taken away from you when in the test room.
- Arrive somewhat ahead of time – If because of transportation schedules you must get there very early, bring a newspaper or magazine to take your mind off yourself while waiting.
- Locate the examination room – When you have found the proper room, you will be directed to the seat or part of the room where you will sit. Sometimes you are given a sheet of instructions to read while you are waiting. Do not fill out any forms until you are told to do so; just read them and be prepared.
- Relax and prepare to listen to the instructions
- If you have any physical problem that may keep you from doing your best, be sure to tell the test administrator. If you are sick or in poor health, you really cannot do your best on the exam. You can come back and take the test some other time.

VII. AT THE TEST

The day of the test is here and you have the test booklet in your hand. The temptation to get going is very strong. Caution! There is more to success than knowing the right answers. You must know how to identify your papers and understand variations in the type of short-answer question used in this particular examination. Follow these suggestions for maximum results from your efforts:

1) Cooperate with the monitor

The test administrator has a duty to create a situation in which you can be as much at ease as possible. He will give instructions, tell you when to begin, check to see that you are marking your answer sheet correctly, and so on. He is not there to guard you, although he will see that your competitors do not take unfair advantage. He wants to help you do your best.

2) Listen to all instructions

Don't jump the gun! Wait until you understand all directions. In most civil service tests you get more time than you need to answer the questions. So don't be in a hurry. Read each word of instructions until you clearly understand the meaning. Study the examples, listen to all announcements and follow directions. Ask questions if you do not understand what to do.

3) Identify your papers

Civil service exams are usually identified by number only. You will be assigned a number; you must not put your name on your test papers. Be sure to copy your number correctly. Since more than one exam may be given, copy your exact examination title.

4) Plan your time

Unless you are told that a test is a "speed" or "rate of work" test, speed itself is usually not important. Time enough to answer all the questions will be provided, but this does not mean that you have all day. An overall time limit has been set. Divide the total time (in minutes) by the number of questions to determine the approximate time you have for each question.

5) Do not linger over difficult questions

If you come across a difficult question, mark it with a paper clip (useful to have along) and come back to it when you have been through the booklet. One caution if you do this – be sure to skip a number on your answer sheet as well. Check often to be sure that you have not lost your place and that you are marking in the row numbered the same as the question you are answering.

6) Read the questions

Be sure you know what the question asks! Many capable people are unsuccessful because they failed to *read* the questions correctly.

7) Answer all questions

Unless you have been instructed that a penalty will be deducted for incorrect answers, it is better to guess than to omit a question.

8) Speed tests

It is often better NOT to guess on speed tests. It has been found that on timed tests people are tempted to spend the last few seconds before time is called in marking answers at random – without even reading them – in the hope of picking up a few extra points. To discourage this practice, the instructions may warn you that your score will be "corrected" for guessing. That is, a penalty will be applied. The incorrect answers will be deducted from the correct ones, or some other penalty formula will be used.

9) Review your answers

If you finish before time is called, go back to the questions you guessed or omitted to give them further thought. Review other answers if you have time.

10) Return your test materials

If you are ready to leave before others have finished or time is called, take ALL your materials to the monitor and leave quietly. Never take any test material with you. The monitor can discover whose papers are not complete, and taking a test booklet may be grounds for disqualification.

VIII. EXAMINATION TECHNIQUES

1) Read the general instructions carefully. These are usually printed on the first page of the exam booklet. As a rule, these instructions refer to the timing of the examination; the fact that you should not start work until the signal and must stop work at a signal, etc. If there are any *special* instructions, such as a choice of questions to be answered, make sure that you note this instruction carefully.

2) When you are ready to start work on the examination, that is as soon as the signal has been given, read the instructions to each question booklet, underline any key words or phrases, such as *least, best, outline, describe* and the like. In this way you will tend to answer as requested rather than discover on reviewing your paper that you *listed without describing*, that you selected the *worst* choice rather than the *best* choice, etc.

3) If the examination is of the objective or multiple-choice type – that is, each question will also give a series of possible answers: A, B, C or D, and you are called upon to select the best answer and write the letter next to that answer on your answer paper – it is advisable to start answering each question in turn. There may be anywhere from 50 to 100 such questions in the three or four hours allotted and you can see how much time would be taken if you read through all the questions before beginning to answer any. Furthermore, if you come across a question or group of questions which you know would be difficult to answer, it would undoubtedly affect your handling of all the other questions.

4) If the examination is of the essay type and contains but a few questions, it is a moot point as to whether you should read all the questions before starting to answer any one. Of course, if you are given a choice – say five out of seven and the like – then it is essential to read all the questions so you can eliminate the two that are most difficult. If, however, you are asked to answer all the questions, there may be danger in trying to answer the easiest one first because you may find that you will spend too much time on it. The best technique is to answer the first question, then proceed to the second, etc.

5) Time your answers. Before the exam begins, write down the time it started, then add the time allowed for the examination and write down the time it must be completed, then divide the time available somewhat as follows:

- If 3-1/2 hours are allowed, that would be 210 minutes. If you have 80 objective-type questions, that would be an average of 2-1/2 minutes per question. Allow yourself no more than 2 minutes per question, or a total of 160 minutes, which will permit about 50 minutes to review.
- If for the time allotment of 210 minutes there are 7 essay questions to answer, that would average about 30 minutes a question. Give yourself only 25 minutes per question so that you have about 35 minutes to review.

6) The most important instruction is to *read each question* and make sure you know what is wanted. The second most important instruction is to *time yourself properly* so that you answer every question. The third most important instruction is to *answer every question*. Guess if you have to but include something for each question. Remember that you will receive no credit for a blank and will probably receive some credit if you write something in answer to an essay question. If you guess a letter – say "B" for a multiple-choice question – you may have guessed right. If you leave a blank as an answer to a multiple-choice question, the examiners may respect your feelings but it will not add a point to your score. Some exams may penalize you for wrong answers, so in such cases *only*, you may not want to guess unless you have some basis for your answer.

7) Suggestions
   a. Objective-type questions
      1. Examine the question booklet for proper sequence of pages and questions
      2. Read all instructions carefully
      3. Skip any question which seems too difficult; return to it after all other questions have been answered
      4. Apportion your time properly; do not spend too much time on any single question or group of questions
      5. Note and underline key words – *all, most, fewest, least, best, worst, same, opposite*, etc.
      6. Pay particular attention to negatives
      7. Note unusual option, e.g., unduly long, short, complex, different or similar in content to the body of the question
      8. Observe the use of "hedging" words – *probably, may, most likely*, etc.
      9. Make sure that your answer is put next to the same number as the question
      10. Do not second-guess unless you have good reason to believe the second answer is definitely more correct
      11. Cross out original answer if you decide another answer is more accurate; do not erase until you are ready to hand your paper in
      12. Answer all questions; guess unless instructed otherwise
      13. Leave time for review

   b. Essay questions
      1. Read each question carefully
      2. Determine exactly what is wanted. Underline key words or phrases.
      3. Decide on outline or paragraph answer

4. Include many different points and elements unless asked to develop any one or two points or elements
5. Show impartiality by giving pros and cons unless directed to select one side only
6. Make and write down any assumptions you find necessary to answer the questions
7. Watch your English, grammar, punctuation and choice of words
8. Time your answers; don't crowd material

8) Answering the essay question

Most essay questions can be answered by framing the specific response around several key words or ideas. Here are a few such key words or ideas:

M's: manpower, materials, methods, money, management
P's: purpose, program, policy, plan, procedure, practice, problems, pitfalls, personnel, public relations

   a. Six basic steps in handling problems:
     1. Preliminary plan and background development
     2. Collect information, data and facts
     3. Analyze and interpret information, data and facts
     4. Analyze and develop solutions as well as make recommendations
     5. Prepare report and sel recommendations
     6. Install recommendations and follow up effectiveness

   b. Pitfalls to avoid
     1. *Taking things for granted* – A statement of the situation does not necessarily imply that each of the elements is necessarily true; for example, a complaint may be invalid and biased so that all that can be taken for granted is that a complaint has been registered
     2. *Considering only one side of a situation* – Wherever possible, indicate several alternatives and then point out the reasons you selected the best one
     3. *Failing to indicate follow up* – Whenever your answer indicates action on your part, make certain that you will take proper follow-up action to see how successful your recommendations, procedures or actions turn out to be
     4. *Taking too long in answering any single question* – Remember to time your answers properly

IX. AFTER THE TEST

Scoring procedures differ in detail among civil service jurisdictions although the general principles are the same. Whether the papers are hand-scored or graded by machine we have described, they are nearly always graded by number. That is, the person who marks the paper knows only the number – never the name – of the applicant. Not until all the papers have been graded will they be matched with names. If other tests, such as training and experience or oral interview ratings have been given, scores will be combined. Different parts of the examination usually have different weights. For example, the written test might count 60 percent of the final grade, and a rating of training and experience 40 percent. In many jurisdictions, veterans will have a certain number of points added to their grades.

After the final grade has been determined, the names are placed in grade order and an eligible list is established. There are various methods for resolving ties between those who get the same final grade – probably the most common is to place first the name of the person whose application was received first. Job offers are made from the eligible list in the order the names appear on it. You will be notified of your grade and your rank as soon as all these computations have been made. This will be done as rapidly as possible.

People who are found to meet the requirements in the announcement are called "eligibles." Their names are put on a list of eligible candidates. An eligible's chances of getting a job depend on how high he stands on this list and how fast agencies are filling jobs from the list.

When a job is to be filled from a list of eligibles, the agency asks for the names of people on the list of eligibles for that job. When the civil service commission receives this request, it sends to the agency the names of the three people highest on this list. Or, if the job to be filled has specialized requirements, the office sends the agency the names of the top three persons who meet these requirements from the general list.

The appointing officer makes a choice from among the three people whose names were sent to him. If the selected person accepts the appointment, the names of the others are put back on the list to be considered for future openings.

That is the rule in hiring from all kinds of eligible lists, whether they are for typist, carpenter, chemist, or something else. For every vacancy, the appointing officer has his choice of any one of the top three eligibles on the list. This explains why the person whose name is on top of the list sometimes does not get an appointment when some of the persons lower on the list do. If the appointing officer chooses the second or third eligible, the No. 1 eligible does not get a job at once, but stays on the list until he is appointed or the list is terminated.

X. HOW TO PASS THE INTERVIEW TEST

The examination for which you applied requires an oral interview test. You have already taken the written test and you are now being called for the interview test – the final part of the formal examination.

You may think that it is not possible to prepare for an interview test and that there are no procedures to follow during an interview. Our purpose is to point out some things you can do in advance that will help you and some good rules to follow and pitfalls to avoid while you are being interviewed.

What is an interview supposed to test?
The written examination is designed to test the technical knowledge and competence of the candidate; the oral is designed to evaluate intangible qualities, not readily measured otherwise, and to establish a list showing the relative fitness of each candidate – as measured against his competitors – for the position sought. Scoring is not on the basis of "right" and "wrong," but on a sliding scale of values ranging from "not passable" to "outstanding." As a matter of fact, it is possible to achieve a relatively low score without a single "incorrect" answer because of evident weakness in the qualities being measured.

Occasionally, an examination may consist entirely of an oral test – either an individual or a group oral. In such cases, information is sought concerning the technical knowledges and abilities of the candidate, since there has been no written examination for this purpose. More commonly, however, an oral test is used to supplement a written examination.

Who conducts interviews?

The composition of oral boards varies among different jurisdictions. In nearly all, a representative of the personnel department serves as chairman. One of the members of the board may be a representative of the department in which the candidate would work. In some cases, "outside experts" are used, and, frequently, a businessman or some other representative of the general public is asked to serve. Labor and management or other special groups may be represented. The aim is to secure the services of experts in the appropriate field.

However the board is composed, it is a good idea (and not at all improper or unethical) to ascertain in advance of the interview who the members are and what groups they represent. When you are introduced to them, you will have some idea of their backgrounds and interests, and at least you will not stutter and stammer over their names.

What should be done before the interview?

While knowledge about the board members is useful and takes some of the surprise element out of the interview, there is other preparation which is more substantive. It *is* possible to prepare for an oral interview – in several ways:

1) Keep a copy of your application and review it carefully before the interview

This may be the only document before the oral board, and the starting point of the interview. Know what education and experience you have listed there, and the sequence and dates of all of it. Sometimes the board will ask you to review the highlights of your experience for them; you should not have to hem and haw doing it.

2) Study the class specification and the examination announcement

Usually, the oral board has one or both of these to guide them. The qualities, characteristics or knowledges required by the position sought are stated in these documents. They offer valuable clues as to the nature of the oral interview. For example, if the job involves supervisory responsibilities, the announcement will usually indicate that knowledge of modern supervisory methods and the qualifications of the candidate as a supervisor will be tested. If so, you can expect such questions, frequently in the form of a hypothetical situation which you are expected to solve. NEVER go into an oral without knowledge of the duties and responsibilities of the job you seek.

3) Think through each qualification required

Try to visualize the kind of questions you would ask if you were a board member. How well could you answer them? Try especially to appraise your own knowledge and background in each area, *measured against the job sought*, and identify any areas in which you are weak. Be critical and realistic – do not flatter yourself.

4) Do some general reading in areas in which you feel you may be weak

For example, if the job involves supervision and your past experience has NOT, some general reading in supervisory methods and practices, particularly in the field of human relations, might be useful. Do NOT study agency procedures or detailed manuals. The oral board will be testing your understanding and capacity, not your memory.

5) Get a good night's sleep and watch your general health and mental attitude

You will want a clear head at the interview. Take care of a cold or any other minor ailment, and of course, no hangovers.

What should be done on the day of the interview?

Now comes the day of the interview itself. Give yourself plenty of time to get there. Plan to arrive somewhat ahead of the scheduled time, particularly if your appointment is in the fore part of the day. If a previous candidate fails to appear, the board might be ready for you a bit early. By early afternoon an oral board is almost invariably behind schedule if there are many candidates, and you may have to wait. Take along a book or magazine to read, or your application to review, but leave any extraneous material in the waiting room when you go in for your interview. In any event, relax and compose yourself.

The matter of dress is important. The board is forming impressions about you – from your experience, your manners, your attitude, and your appearance. Give your personal appearance careful attention. Dress your best, but not your flashiest. Choose conservative, appropriate clothing, and be sure it is immaculate. This is a business interview, and your appearance should indicate that you regard it as such. Besides, being well groomed and properly dressed will help boost your confidence.

Sooner or later, someone will call your name and escort you into the interview room. *This is it.* From here on you are on your own. It is too late for any more preparation. But remember, you asked for this opportunity to prove your fitness, and you are here because your request was granted.

What happens when you go in?

The usual sequence of events will be as follows: The clerk (who is often the board stenographer) will introduce you to the chairman of the oral board, who will introduce you to the other members of the board. Acknowledge the introductions before you sit down. Do not be surprised if you find a microphone facing you or a stenotypist sitting by. Oral interviews are usually recorded in the event of an appeal or other review.

Usually the chairman of the board will open the interview by reviewing the highlights of your education and work experience from your application – primarily for the benefit of the other members of the board, as well as to get the material into the record. Do not interrupt or comment unless there is an error or significant misinterpretation; if that is the case, do not hesitate. But do not quibble about insignificant matters. Also, he will usually ask you some question about your education, experience or your present job – partly to get you to start talking and to establish the interviewing "rapport." He may start the actual questioning, or turn it over to one of the other members. Frequently, each member undertakes the questioning on a particular area, one in which he is perhaps most competent, so you can expect each member to participate in the examination. Because time is limited, you may also expect some rather abrupt switches in the direction the questioning takes, so do not be upset by it. Normally, a board member will not pursue a single line of questioning unless he discovers a particular strength or weakness.

After each member has participated, the chairman will usually ask whether any member has any further questions, then will ask you if you have anything you wish to add. Unless you are expecting this question, it may floor you. Worse, it may start you off on an extended, extemporaneous speech. The board is not usually seeking more information. The question is principally to offer you a last opportunity to present further qualifications or to indicate that you have nothing to add. So, if you feel that a significant qualification or characteristic has been overlooked, it is proper to point it out in a sentence or so. Do not compliment the board on the thoroughness of their examination – they have been sketchy, and you know it. If you wish, merely say, "No thank you, I have nothing further to add." This is a point where you can "talk yourself out" of a good impression or fail to present an important bit of information. Remember, *you close the interview yourself.*

The chairman will then say, "That is all, Mr. _____, thank you." Do not be startled; the interview is over, and quicker than you think. Thank him, gather your belongings and take your leave. Save your sigh of relief for the other side of the door.

How to put your best foot forward

Throughout this entire process, you may feel that the board individually and collectively is trying to pierce your defenses, seek out your hidden weaknesses and embarrass and confuse you. Actually, this is not true. They are obliged to make an appraisal of your qualifications for the job you are seeking, and they want to see you in your best light. Remember, they must interview all candidates and a non-cooperative candidate may become a failure in spite of their best efforts to bring out his qualifications. Here are 15 suggestions that will help you:

1) Be natural – Keep your attitude confident, not cocky

If you are not confident that you can do the job, do not expect the board to be. Do not apologize for your weaknesses, try to bring out your strong points. The board is interested in a positive, not negative, presentation. Cockiness will antagonize any board member and make him wonder if you are covering up a weakness by a false show of strength.

2) Get comfortable, but don't lounge or sprawl

Sit erectly but not stiffly. A careless posture may lead the board to conclude that you are careless in other things, or at least that you are not impressed by the importance of the occasion. Either conclusion is natural, even if incorrect. Do not fuss with your clothing, a pencil or an ashtray. Your hands may occasionally be useful to emphasize a point; do not let them become a point of distraction.

3) Do not wisecrack or make small talk

This is a serious situation, and your attitude should show that you consider it as such. Further, the time of the board is limited – they do not want to waste it, and neither should you.

4) Do not exaggerate your experience or abilities

In the first place, from information in the application or other interviews and sources, the board may know more about you than you think. Secondly, you probably will not get away with it. An experienced board is rather adept at spotting such a situation, so do not take the chance.

5) If you know a board member, do not make a point of it, yet do not hide it

Certainly you are not fooling him, and probably not the other members of the board. Do not try to take advantage of your acquaintanceship – it will probably do you little good.

6) Do not dominate the interview

Let the board do that. They will give you the clues – do not assume that you have to do all the talking. Realize that the board has a number of questions to ask you, and do not try to take up all the interview time by showing off your extensive knowledge of the answer to the first one.

7) Be attentive

You only have 20 minutes or so, and you should keep your attention at its sharpest throughout. When a member is addressing a problem or question to you, give him your undivided attention. Address your reply principally to him, but do not exclude the other board members.

8) Do not interrupt

A board member may be stating a problem for you to analyze. He will ask you a question when the time comes. Let him state the problem, and wait for the question.

9) Make sure you understand the question

Do not try to answer until you are sure what the question is. If it is not clear, restate it in your own words or ask the board member to clarify it for you. However, do not haggle about minor elements.

10) Reply promptly but not hastily

A common entry on oral board rating sheets is "candidate responded readily," or "candidate hesitated in replies." Respond as promptly and quickly as you can, but do not jump to a hasty, ill-considered answer.

11) Do not be peremptory in your answers

A brief answer is proper – but do not fire your answer back. That is a losing game from your point of view. The board member can probably ask questions much faster than you can answer them.

12) Do not try to create the answer you think the board member wants

He is interested in what kind of mind you have and how it works – not in playing games. Furthermore, he can usually spot this practice and will actually grade you down on it.

13) Do not switch sides in your reply merely to agree with a board member

Frequently, a member will take a contrary position merely to draw you out and to see if you are willing and able to defend your point of view. Do not start a debate, yet do not surrender a good position. If a position is worth taking, it is worth defending.

14) Do not be afraid to admit an error in judgment if you are shown to be wrong

The board knows that you are forced to reply without any opportunity for careful consideration. Your answer may be demonstrably wrong. If so, admit it and get on with the interview.

15) Do not dwell at length on your present job

The opening question may relate to your present assignment. Answer the question but do not go into an extended discussion. You are being examined for a *new* job, not your present one. As a matter of fact, try to phrase ALL your answers in terms of the job for which you are being examined.

Basis of Rating

Probably you will forget most of these "do's" and "don'ts" when you walk into the oral interview room. Even remembering them all will not ensure you a passing grade. Perhaps you did not have the qualifications in the first place. But remembering them will help you to put your best foot forward, without treading on the toes of the board members.

Rumor and popular opinion to the contrary notwithstanding, an oral board wants you to make the best appearance possible. They know you are under pressure – but they also want to see how you respond to it as a guide to what your reaction would be under the pressures of the job you seek. They will be influenced by the degree of poise you display, the personal traits you show and the manner in which you respond.

ABOUT THIS BOOK

This book contains tests divided into Examination Sections. Go through each test, answering every question in the margin. At the end of each test look at the answer key and check your answers. On the ones you got wrong, look at the right answer choice and learn. Do not fill in the answers first. Do not memorize the questions and answers, but understand the answer and principles involved. On your test, the questions will likely be different from the samples. Questions are changed and new ones added. If you understand these past questions you should have success with any changes that arise. Tests may consist of several types of questions. We have additional books on each subject should more study be advisable or necessary for you. Finally, the more you study, the better prepared you will be. This book is intended to be the last thing you study before you walk into the examination room. Prior study of relevant texts is also recommended. NLC publishes some of these in our Fundamental Series. Knowledge and good sense are important factors in passing your exam. Good luck also helps. So now study this Passbook, absorb the material contained within and take that knowledge into the examination. Then do your best to pass that exam.

EXAMINATION SECTION

BOOKKEEPING PROBLEMS
EXAMINATION SECTION
TEST 1

DIRECTIONS: Each question or incomplete statement is followed by several suggested answers or completions. Select the one that BEST answers the question or completes the statement. *PRINT THE LETTER OF THE CORRECT ANSWER IN THE SPACE AT THE RIGHT.*

1. The accounts in a general ledger are BEST arranged   1._____

    A. in numerical order
    B. according to the frequency with which each account is used
    C. according to the order in which the headings of the columns in the cash journals are arranged
    D. according to the order in which they are used in preparing financial statements

2. A physical inventory is an inventory obtained by   2._____

    A. an actual count of the items on hand
    B. adding the totals of the stock record cards
    C. deducting the cost of goods sold from the purchases for the period
    D. deducting the purchases from the sales for the period

3. Modern accounting practice favors the valuation of the inventories of a going concern at   3._____

    A. current market prices, if higher than cost
    B. cost or market, whichever is lower
    C. estimated selling price
    D. probable value at forced sale

4. A subsidiary ledger contains accounts which show   4._____

    A. details of contingent liabilities of undetermined amount
    B. totals of all asset accounts in the general ledger
    C. totals of all liability accounts in the general ledger
    D. details of an account in the general ledger

5. A statement of the assets, liabilities, and net worth of a business is called a   5._____

    A. trial balance   B. budget
    C. profit and loss statement   D. balance sheet

6. The one of the following which is NEVER properly considered a negotiable instrument is a(n)   6._____

    A. invoice   B. bond
    C. promissory note   D. endorsed check

7. The term *current assets* USUALLY includes such things as   7._____

    A. notes payable   B. machinery and equipment
    C. furniture and fixtures   D. accounts receivable

8. An accounting system which records revenues as soon as they are earned and records   8.____
liabilities as soon as they are incurred regardless of the date of payment is said to operate on a(n) _____ basis.

    A. accrual   B. budgetary   C. encumbrance   D. cash

9. A *trial balance* is a list of   9.____

    A. the credit balances in all accounts in a general ledger
    B. all general ledger accounts and their balances
    C. the asset accounts in a general ledger and their balances
    D. the liability accounts in a general ledger and their balances

10. A controlling account contains the totals of   10.____

    A. the accounts used in preparing the balance sheet at the end of the fiscal period
    B. the individual amounts entered in the accounts of a subsidiary ledger during the
        fiscal period
    C. all entries in the general journal during the fiscal period
    D. the accounts used in preparing the profit and loss statement for the fiscal period

11. The ESSENTIAL nature of an asset is that it(s)   11.____

    A. must be tangible
    B. must be easily converted into cash
    C. must have value
    D. cost must be included in the profit and loss statement

12. When an asset is depreciated on the straight-line basis, the amount charged off for   12.____
depreciation

    A. is greater in the earlier years of the asset's life
    B. is greater in the later years of the asset's life
    C. varies each year according to the extent to which the asset is used during the year
    D. is equal each full year of the asset's life

Questions 13-27.

DIRECTIONS: Questions 13 to 27 consist of a list of some of the accounts in a general ledger.
Indicate whether each account listed generally contains a debit or a credit balance by putting the letter D (for debit balance) or the letter C (for credit balance) in the correspondingly numbered space on the right for each account
listed. For example, for the account Cash, which generally contains a debit balance, you would give the letter D as your answer.

13. Sales Taxes Collected   13.____

14. Social Security Taxes Paid by Employer   14.____

15. Deposits from Customers   15.____

16. Freight Inward   16.____

17. Sales Discount   17.____

18. Withholding Taxes Payable   18.____

19. L. Norton, Drawings   19.____

20. Office Salaries   20.____

21. Merchandise Inventory   21.____

22. L. Norton, Capital   22.____

23. Purchases Returns   23.____

24. Unearned Rent Income   24.____

25. Reserve for Bad Debts   25.____

26. Depreciation of Machinery   26.____

27. Insurance Prepaid   27.____

Questions 28-42.

DIRECTIONS: Questions 28 to 42 consist of a list of some of the accounts in a general ledger. For the purpose of preparing financial statements, each of these accounts is to be classified into one of the following five major classifications, lettered A to E, as follows:

A. Assets   B. Liabilities   C. Proprietorship
D. Income   E. Expense

You are to indicate the classification to which each account belongs by printing the correct letter, A, E, C, D, or E, in the correspondingly numbered space on the right. For example, for the account Furniture and Fixtures, which is an asset account, you would print the letter A.

28. Notes Receivable   28.____

29. Sales   29.____

30. Wages Payable   30.____

31. Office Salaries   31.____

32. Capital Stock Authorized   32.____

33. Goodwill   33.____

34. Capital Surplus   34.____

35. Office Supplies Used   35.____

36. Interest Payable   36.____

37. Prepaid Rent   37.____

38. Interest Cost   38.____

39. Accounts Payable   39.____

40. Prepaid Insurance   40.____

41. Merchandise Inventory   41.____

42. Interest Earned   42.____

43. A trial balance will NOT indicate that an error has been made in   43.____

     A. computing the balance of an account
     B. entering an amount in the wrong account
     C. carrying forward the balance of an account
     D. entering an amount on the wrong side of an account

44. Many business firms maintain a book of original entry in which all bills to be paid are recorded.   44.____
This book is known as a

     A. purchase returns journal   B. subsidiary ledger
     C. voucher register   D. notes payable register

45. Many business firms provide a petty cash fund from which to pay for small items in order to avoid the issuing of many small checks.   45.____
If this fund is replenished periodically to restore it to its original amount, the fund is called a(n) _____ fund.

     A. imprest   B. debenture
     C. adjustment   D. expense reserve

46. A firm which voluntarily terminates business, selling its assets and paying its liabilities, is said to be in   46.____

     A. receivership   B. liquidation
     C. depletion   D. amortization

47. The phrase *3%-10 days* on an invoice ORDINARILY means that   47.____

     A. 3% of the amount must be paid each 10 days
     B. the purchaser is entitled to only ten days credit
     C. a discount of 3% will be allowed for payment in 10 days
     D. the entire amount must be paid in 10 days or a penalty of 3% of the amount due will be added

48. The CHIEF disadvantage of *single-entry* bookkeeping is that it   48.____

     A. is too difficult to operate
     B. is illegal for income tax purposes
     C. provides no possibility of determining net profits
     D. furnishes an incomplete picture of the business

49. Sales *minus* cost of goods sold *equals*   49.____

     A. net profit   B. gross sales
     C. gross profit   D. net sales

50. The amounts of the transactions recorded in a journal are transferred to the general ledger accounts by a process known as
    50.____

    A. auditing   B. balancing   C. posting   D. verifying

51. A merchant purchased a stock of goods and priced these goods so as to gain 40% on the cost to him.
    51.____
If the merchant sold these goods for $840, the COST of these goods to him was

    A. $556   B. $600   C. $348   D. $925

52. In the interest at 6% for one full year on a principal sum amounts to $12, the *principal sum* is
    52.____

    A. $150   B. $96   C. $196   D. $200

53. On October 17, a business man discounted a customer's 90-day non-interest bearing note at his bank. The face of the note was $960, and it was dated September 28. The discount rate was 5%.
    53.____
Using a 360-day year, the amount in cash that the business man received from the bank was MOST NEARLY

    A. $899.33   B. $950.67   C. $967.50   D. $989.75

54. A certain correctly totaled cash receipts journal contained the following columns: Net Cash Debit, Accounts Receivable, Sales Discounts, and General.
    54.____
At the end of April, the totals of the columns were as follows: Net Cash Debit - $18,925.15, Accounts Receivable (not given), Sales Discounts - $379.65, General - $5,639.25.
The TOTAL of the Accounts Receivable column was

    A. $11,194.50   B. $21 344.32   C. $7,621.19   D. $13,665.55

55. In its first year of operation, a retail store had cash sales of $49,000 and installment sales of $41,000.
    55.____
If 12% of the amount of these installment sales were collected in that year, the TOTAL amount of cash received from sales was

    A. $22,176   B. $34,987   C. $53,920   D. $55,650

56. I. Conklin and J. Ulster formed a partnership and agreed to share profits in proportion to their initial capital investments. I. Conklin invested $15,000 and J. Ulster invested $12,500.
    56.____
If the profits for the year were $16,500, J. Ulster's share of the profits was

    A. $6,750   B. $7,500   C. $8,100   D. $8,300

57. In a certain city, the tax rate on real estate one year was $48.75 per thousand dollars of assessed valuation. If an apartment house in that city was assessed for $185,000, the real estate tax payable by the owner of that house was MOST NEARLY
    57.____

    A. $9,018.75   B. $9,009.75   C. $8,900.00   D. $8,905.25

58. A correctly totaled cash payments journal contained the following columns: Net Cash,   58.____
Accounts Payable, Purchase Discounts, General.
At the end of April, the totals of the columns were as follows: Net Cash - $18,375.60,
Accounts Payable - $16,981.19, Purchase Discounts (not given), General - $1,875.37.
The TOTAL of the Purchase Discounts column was

  A. $120.36   B. $239.87   C. $480.96   D. $670.51

59. On January 1, the credit balance of the Accounts Payable account in a general ledger   59.____
was $9,139.87. For the month of January, the Purchase Journal total amounted to
$3,467.81; the Accounts Payable column in the Cash Disbursements Journal amounted
to $2,935.55; the total of the Returned Purchases Journal for January amounted to
$173.15; and the Miscellaneous column in the Cash Disbursements Journal showed that
$750 had been paid in January on notes given to creditors and entered in previous
months.
The BALANCE in the Accounts Payable account at the end of January was

  A. $8,437.89   B. $9,498.98   C. $9,998.98   D. $10,132.68

60. The bank statement received from his bank by a business man showed a certain balance   60.____
for the month of June. This bank statement showed a service charge of $5.19 for the
month. He discovered that a check drawn by him in the amount of $83.75 and returned
by the bank had been entered on the stub of his checkbook as $38.75. He also found
that two checks which he had issued, #29 for $37.18 and #33 for $18.69, were not listed
on the statement and had not been returned by the bank. The balance in his checkbook
before he reconciled it with the balance shown on the bank statement was $8,917.91.
The BALANCE on the bank statement was

  A. $8,903.97   B. $8,923.59   C. $8,997.65   D. $9,303.95

KEY (CORRECT ANSWERS)

1.	D	16.	D	31.	E	46.	B
2.	A	17.	D	32.	C	47.	C
3.	B	18.	C	33.	A	48.	D
4.	D	19.	D	34.	C	49.	C
5.	D	20.	D	35.	E	50.	C
6.	A	21.	D	36.	B	51.	B
7.	D	22.	C	37.	A	52.	D
8.	A	23.	C	38.	E	53.	B
9.	B	24.	C	39.	B	54.	D
10.	B	25.	C	40.	A	55.	C
11.	C	26.	D	41.	A	56.	B
12.	D	27.	D	42.	D	57.	A
13.	C	28.	A	43.	B	58.	C
14.	D	29.	D	44.	C	59.	B
15.	C	30.	B	45.	A	60.	B

TEST 2

Questions 1-25.

DIRECTIONS: 1. Below you will find the general ledger balances on February 28 in the books of C. Dutton.
2. On the following pages, you will find all the entries on the books of C. Dutton for the month of March.
3. In the appropriate spaces on the right, you are to supply the new balances for the accounts called for at the end of March.

The correct balances in the general ledger of C. Dutton on February 28 were as follows: (NOTE: The accounts below have not been arranged in the customary trial balance form.)

Cash	$4,336
Accounts Receivable	8,165
Notes Receivable	2,200
Furniture and Fixtures	9,000
Merchandise Inventory 1/1	4,175
Accounts Payable	5,560
Notes Payable	1,500
Reserve for Depreciation of Furniture and Fixtures	1,800
C. Dutton, Capital	14,162
C. Dutton, Drawing	900
Purchases	42,600
Freight In	36
Rent	1,750
Light	126
Telephone	63
Salaries	4,076
Shipping Expenses	368
Sales	53,200
Sales Biscount	637
Purchase Biscount	596
City Sales Tax Collected	804
Social Security Taxes Payable	96
Withholding Taxes Payable	714

CASH RECEIPTS

Date	Name	Net Cash	Accounts Receivable	Sales Disc.	Miscellaneous Acct.	Amount
3/1	T. Blint	6,027.00	6,150.00	123.00		
	K . Crowe	1,015.00			Notes Rec.	1,000.00
					Int. Income	15.00
3/10	N. Tandy	3,969.00	4,050.00	81.00		
3/17	Rebuilt Desk Co.	45.00			Furn. & Fixt.	45.00
3/24	J. Walter	2,910.00	3,000.00	90.00		
3/31	National Federal Bank	3,000.00			Notes Payable	3,000.00
		16,966.00	13,200.00	294.00		4,060.00

7

CASH DISBURSEMENTS

Date		Net Cash	Accts. Pay.	Purch Disc.	Soc. Sec. Tax	With-hold Tax	Miscellaneous Acct .	Amount
3/1	Bliss Realty Co.	875.00					Rent	875.00
3/4	Con. Edison	54.00					Light	54.00
3/10	D. LaRue	2,891.00	2,950.00	59.00				
3/15	Payroll	747.00			26.00	175.	Sal.	948.00
3/19	Rebuilt Desk Co.	115.00					Furn/Fixt	115.00
3/26	Jiggs & Co.	3,686.00	3,800.00	114.00				
3/30	Nat'l Fed Bank	1,218.00					Notes Pay.	1200.00
							Int. Cost	18.00
3/31	Payroll	733.00			22.00	171.	Salary	926.00
3/31	C. Dutton	600.00					Draw	600.00
		10,919.00	6,750.00	173.00	48.00	346.00		4736.00

SALES BOOK

Date	Name	Accts. Rec.	Sales	City Sales Tax
3/3	K . Crowe	6,850.00	6,665.00	185.00
3/10	J. Walters	5,730.00	5,730.00	
3/16	N. Tandy	3,100.00	3,007.00	93.00
3/25	Willis & Co.	7,278.00	7,069.00	209.00
3/30	V. Clyburne	2,190.00	2,190.00	
		25,148.00	24,661.00	487.00

PURCHASE BOOK

Date		Accts. Pay.	Purchases	Freight In	Miscellaneous Acct .	Amount
3/4	Jiggs & Co.	5,212.00	5,070.00	142.00		
3/11	Barton & Co.	320.00			Ins. Prepd.	320.00
3/16	A. Field	6,368.00	6,179.00	189.00		
3/19	Smith Delivery	22.00			Ship. Exp.	22.00
3/23	N.Y. Telephone	29.00			Telephone	29.00
3/26	D . LaRue	3,000.00	3,000.00			
3/29	App & App	7,531.00	7,168.00	363.00		
		22,482.00	21,417.00	694.00		371.00

Supply the balances of the following accounts on March 31 after all posting has been done for March. Put answers in the appropriate spaces on the right. Give amounts only.

1. Cash

2. Accounts Receivable

3. Notes Receivable

4. Insurance Prepaid

5. Furniture and Fixtures

6. Accounts Payable

7. Notes Payable

1.____

2.____

3.____

4.____

5.____

6.____

7.____

8. Reserve for Depreciation of Furniture and Fixtures   8._____

9. C. Dutton, Capital   9._____

10. C. Dutton, Drawing   10._____

11. Purchases   11._____

12. Freight In   12._____

13. Rent   13._____

14. Light   14._____

15. Telephone   15._____

16. Salaries   16._____

17. Shipping Expenses   17._____

18. Sales   18._____

19. Sales Discount   19._____

20. Purchase Discount   20._____

21. City Sales Tax Collected   21._____

22. Social Security Taxes Payable   22._____

23. Withholding Taxes Payable   23._____

24. Interest Income   24._____

25. Interest Cost   25._____

Questions 26-35.

DIRECTIONS: Mr. Adams has a complete set of books - Cash Journals, Purchase and Sales Journals, and a General Journal. Below you will find the General Journal used by Mr. Adams. Under the heading of each money column, you will find a letter of the alphabet. Following the General Journal, there is a series of transactions. You are to determine the correct entry for each transaction and then show on the right in the appropriate space the columns to be used. For example, if a certain transaction results in an entry of $100 in the Notes Receiving Column (on the left side) and an entry of $100 in the General Ledger Column (on the right side), in the appropriate space on the right, you should write A, D. If the record of the transaction requires the use of more than two columns, your answer should contain more than two letters. DO NOT PUT THE AMOUNTS IN YOUR ANSWER SPACE. The LETTERS of the columns to be used are sufficient. If a transaction requires no entry in the General Journal, write None in the appropriate space in your answer space, even though a record would be made in some other journal.

GENERAL JOURNAL

Notes Receivable	Accounts Payable	General Ledger	L. F.		General Ledger	Accounts Receivable	Notes Payable
A	B	C			D	E	F

26. We sent Tripp & Co. a 30-day trade acceptance for $500 for merchandise sold him today. They accepted it.   26.____

27. The proprietor, Mr. Adams, returned $100 in cash to be deposited, representing Traveling Expenses he had not used.   27.____

28. An entry in the purchase journal last month for a purchase invoice from V. Valides for $647 was erroneously entered in the purchase journal as $746 and posted as such.   28.____

29. A check for $200 received from Mr. Breen was erroneously credited to account of P. Ungar.   29.____

30. In posting the totals of the cash receipts journal last month, an item of bank discount of $30 on our note for $1500 discounted for 60 days was included in the total posted to the sales discount account.   30.____

31. M. Hogan paid his note of $600 and interest of $12 and his account was credited for $612.   31.____

32. Mr. Blow informed us he could not pay his invoice of $2000 due today. Instead, he sent us his 30-day note for $2000 for 30 days bearing interest at 6% per annum.   32.____

33. The proprietor, Mr. Adams, drew $75 to buy his daughter a U.S. Bond.   33.____

34. Mr. O'Brien wrote to us that we overcharged him on an invoice last week.   34.____

35. Returned $120 worth of merchandise to Pecora & Co. and received their credit memorandum.   35.____

Questions 36-50.

DIRECTIONS: In Questions 36 to 50, you will find a list of accounts with a number before each.

1. Cash
2. Accounts Receivable
3. Notes Receivable
4. Notes Receivable Discounted
5. Furniture and Fixtures
6. Delivery Equipment
7. Insurance Prepaid
8. Depreciation on Delivery Equipment
9. Bad Debts
10. Purchases
11. Discount on Purchases
12. Sales

13. Discount on Sales
14. Accounts Payable
15. Notes Payable
16. Interest Cost
17. Reserve for Depreciation on Delivery Equipment
18. Reserve for Bad Debts
19. Sales Taxes Collected
20. Ben Miller, Capital
21. Ben Miller, Drawing
22. Interest Income
23. Purchase Returns

Using the number in front of each account title (using no accounts not listed), make journal entries for the transactions given below. Do not write the names of the accounts in your answer space. Simply indicate in the proper space on the right the numbers of the accounts to be debited or credited. Always give the number or numbers of the accounts to be debited first, then give the number or numbers of accounts to be credited. For example, if furniture and fixtures and delivery equipment are to be debited, and cash and notes payable are to be credited in a certain transaction, then write in your answer space 5, 6 - 1, 15 (use a dash to separate the debits from the credits).

36. F. Pierce, a customer, went into bankruptcy owing us $600. We received a check for $200.　　36.＿＿＿

37. Later in the month, we are informed that there is no possibility of collecting the balance from F. Pierce. There is a sufficient balance in the Reserve for Bad Debts to take care of the above.　　37.＿＿＿

38. Set up the Depreciation on the Delivery Equipment for the year amounting to $240.　　38.＿＿＿

39. Discounted M. Colby's note for $500 today and received $490 in proceeds.　　39.＿＿＿

40. Mr. Miller, the proprietor, invested $2000 in the business.　　40.＿＿＿

41. Paid our note due to Dillon & Co. today for $800 with interest of $16.　　41.＿＿＿

42. Accepted Finnegan's trade acceptance for $1500 for merchandise bought today.　　42.＿＿＿

43. Create a Reserve for Bad Debts of $2000 at the end of the year.　　43.＿＿＿

44. Returned to Dillon & Co. $30 worth of damaged merchandise for credit. They allowed it.　　44.＿＿＿

45. G. Garry claimed a discount of $12 which we had failed to allow him. He had already paid his bill. Sent him check for $12.　　45.＿＿＿

46. On one sale during the month, we had failed to collect the Sales Tax of $15. Wrote to the customer and he sent us a check for $15.　　46.＿＿＿

47. M. Colby paid his note due today which we had discounted two months ago.　　47.＿＿＿

48. Bought a new safe for $875 from Cramer & Co., terms 2/10, n/60 days. Agreed to pay them in 60 days.　　48.＿＿＿

49. Bought merchandise during the month amounting to $17,500 - all on account.　　49.＿＿＿

50. On December 31, paid for a Fire Insurance policy to run for three years from that date - premium was $480.　　50.＿＿＿

51. The following information was taken from the ledger of Peter Dolan on Dec. 31 after adjusting entries had been posted to the ledger.　　51.＿＿＿

Sales Income	$60,000
Sales Returns	3,500
Mdse. Purchases	42,000
Inventory of 1/1	9,400
Sales Taxes Payable	360
Freight Inward	225
Inventory 12/31	7,640
Insurance Unexpired	163

Find the gross profit on Sales for the year.

52. On March 31, your bank sent you a statement of account. You compared the canceled checks with the stubs in your checkbook and found the following:
    Check #34 - $56.00 had not been paid by the bank
    #44 - $38.00 had been paid by the bank as $38.89 because the amount on the check did not agree with your stub in the checkbook
    #52 - $76.50 had not been returned by the bank, though the check had been certified
    #57 - $127.42 had not been paid by the bank
    What total amount would you deduct from the balance on the bank's statement as checks outstanding?
    52.____

53. On April 30, Mr. Jolley received his statement of account from the bank. A comparison of the bank statement and your checkbook revealed the following: Checkbook balance $5,640; this included a deposit of $325 on the last day of April which had not been entered on the bank statement.
    You also find the following:
    Check #69 - $89.00 had not been paid by the bank
    #70 - Paid by the bank as $47.55, had been entered in your checkbook as $45.57
    #76 - $114.30 had not been paid by the bank
    The bank statement included a debit memo of $4.00 for excessive activity during the month.
    What was the balance on the bank statement?
    53.____

54. An invoice dated January 15 for merchandise you bought added up to $876.00. The terms were 3/10, n/60, F.O.B. DESTINATION. When the goods arrived, you paid freight amounting to $8.50. On January 20, you returned goods billed at $26 and received credit therefor. You paid the bill on January 24.
    What was the amount of your check?
    54.____

55. Income taxes paid by residents of a certain state are based on the balance of taxable income at the following
    rates: 2% on first $1000 or less
    3% on 2nd and 3rd $1000
    4% on 4th and 5th $1000
    5% on 6th and 7th $1000
    6% on 8th and 9th $1000
    7% on all over $9000
    What would be the NORMAL income tax to be paid by a resident of that state whose taxable balance of income was $6,750?
    55.____

56. A salesman's gross earnings for the year came to $8,820. His rate of Commission was 5% of his sales to customers after deducting returns by customers. During the year, his customers returned 10% of the goods they purchased. What were his total sales during the year before deducting returns?
    56.____

57. On December 31, the insurance account contained a debit for $144 for a three-year fire insurance policy dated August 1. What amount should be listed on the balance sheet of December 31 of that year?
    57.____

58. A partnership began business on January 1 with partners' investments of $26,000. During the year, the partners drew $ 8,500 for personal use. On December 31, the assets of the firm were $46,300, and the liabilities were $15,600. What was the firm's net profit for the year? (Write P or L before your answer.)   58.____

59. The rent income account of a real estate firm showed a total balance of $75,640 at the end of 1986. Of this amount, $3,545 represented prepaid 1987 rents. The account also included entries for 1986 rents due from tenants but not yet collected, amounting to $2,400.
What amount should be listed on the profit and loss statement as rent income for 1986?   59.____

60. You discounted a customer's note for $7,200 at your bank at the rate of 6% and received net proceeds of $7,182.
How many days did the note have to run from date of discount to date of maturity? (Use 360 days to the year.)   60.____

Questions 61-90.

DIRECTIONS: In Questions 61 to 90, you will find a list of ledger accounts. Indicate whether an account is generally listed in the Trial Balance as a DEBIT or as a CREDIT by putting the letter *D* or the letter *C* in the correct space on the right for each account listed.

61. Sales   61.____

62. Land   62.____

63. Notes Payable   63.____

64. Traveling Expenses   64.____

65. Purchases   65.____

66. Buildings   66.____

67. Merchandise Inventory   67.____

68. Machinery and Equipment   68.____

69. Notes Receivable   69.____

70. Bonds Payable   70.____

71. Advertising   71.____

72. Delivery Expense   72.____

73. Cash   73.____

74. Accounts Payable   74.____

75. Interest on Bonds   75.____

76. Real Estate Taxes   76.____

77. Accounts Receivable   77.____

78. Don Burch, Proprietor   78.____

79. Sales Discount   79.____

80. Withholding Taxes   80.____

81. Depreciation   81.____

82. Prepaid Insurance   82.____

83. Reserve for Dep. on Buildings   83.____

84. Rent Income   84.____

85. Reserve for Bad Debts   85.____

86. Don Burch, Drawing Account   86.____

87. Sales Returns   87.____

88. Bad Debts   88.____

89. Purchase Discount   89.____

90. Reserve for Dep. on Machinery & Equipment   90.____

_____

KEY (CORRECT ANSWERS)

1.	$ 10,383	31.	C,D,D	61.	C
2.	$ 20,113	32.	A,E	62.	D
3.	$ 1,200	33.	None	63.	C
4.	$ 320	34.	C,E	64.	D
5.	$ 9,070	35.	B,D	65.	D
6.	$ 21,292	36.	1-2	66.	D
7.	$ 3,300	37.	18-2	67.	D
8.	$ 1,800	38.	8-17	68.	D
9.	$ 14,162	39.	1,16-4	69.	D
10.	$ 1,500	40.	1-20	70.	C
11.	$ 64,017	41.	15,16-1	71.	D
12.	$ 730	42.	14-15	72.	D
13.	$ 2,625	43.	9-18	73.	D
14.	$ 180	44.	14-23	74.	C
15.	$ 92	45.	13-1	75.	D
16.	$ 5,950	46.	1-19	76.	D
17.	$ 390	47.	4-3	77.	D
18.	$ 77,861	48.	5-14	78.	C
19.	$ 931	49.	10-14	79.	D
20.	$ 769	50.	7-1	80.	C
21.	$ 1,291	51.	$12,515	81.	D
22.	$ 144	52.	$ 183.42	82.	D
23.	$ 1,060	53.	$ 5,512.32	83.	C
24.	$ 15	54.	$ 816	84.	C
25.	$ 18	55.	$ 247.50	85.	C
26.	A-E	56.	$196,000	86.	D
27.	None	57.	$ 124	87.	D
28.	B-D	58.	P $23,200	88.	D
29.	C,E	59.	$72,095	89.	C
30.	C,D	60.	15	90.	C

TEST 3

DIRECTIONS: Each question or incomplete statement is followed by several suggested answers or completions. Select the one that BEST answers the question or completes the statement. *PRINT THE LETTER OF THE CORRECT ANSWER IN THE SPACE AT THE RIGHT.*

1. Of the following taxes, the one which is levied MOST NEARLY in accordance with ability to pay is a(n) _____ tax.

   A. excise
   B. income
   C. general property
   D. sales

1.____

2. When a check has been lost, the bank on which it is drawn should ORDINARILY be notified and instructed to

   A. stop payment on the check
   B. issue a duplicate of the check
   C. charge the account of the drawer for the amount of the check
   D. certify the check

2.____

3. The profit and loss statement prepared for a retail store does NOT ordinarily show

   A. the cost of goods sold
   B. depreciation of fixtures and equipment
   C. expenditures for salaries of employees
   D. the net worth of the proprietor

3.____

4. When two business corporations join their assets and liabilities to form a new corporation, the procedures is called a(n)

   A. merger
   B. liquidation
   C. receivership
   D. exchange

4.____

5. The method of depreciation which deducts an equal amount each full year of an asset's life is called _____ depreciation.

   A. sum-of-years digits
   B. declining balance
   C. straight-line
   D. service-hours

5.____

6. A fixed asset is an asset that

   A. is held primarily for sale to customers
   B. is used in the conduct of the business until worn out or replaced
   C. is readily convertible into cash
   D. has no definite value

6.____

7. The gross profit on sales for a period is determined by

   A. subtracting the cost of goods sold from the sales
   B. subtracting the sales returns and the discounts on sales from the gross sales
   C. subtracting the sales from the purchases for the period
   D. finding the difference between the inventory of merchandise at the beginning of the period and the inventory of merchandise at the end of the period

7.____

16

8. The term *auditing* refers to the 8.____

    A. entering of amounts from the journals into the general ledger
    B. reconciliation of the accounts in a subsidiary ledger with the controlling account in the general ledger
    C. preparation of a trial balance of the accounts in the general ledger
    D. examination of the general ledger and other records of a concern to determine its true financial condition

9. A voucher register is a 9.____

    A. type of electric cash register
    B. list of customers whose accounts are past due
    C. list of the assets of a business
    D. book in which bills to be paid are recorded

10. The account DISCOUNT ON PURCHASES is *properly* closed directly to the _____ account. 10.____

    A. Accounts Payable   B. Sales
    C. Purchases   D. Fixtures

11. The account UNEARNED RENTAL INCOME is *usually* considered a(n) _____ account. 11.____

    A. asset   B. nominal   C. capital   D. liability

12. A controlling account is an account which contains 12.____

    A. the totals of *all* the expense accounts in the general ledger
    B. the total of the amounts entered in the accounts in a subsidiary ledger
    C. the total of the depreciation on fixtures claimed in *all* preceding years
    D. *all* totals of the income and expense accounts before closing to the Profit and Loss account

13. The purpose of the DRAWING account in the general ledger of an individual enterprise is to show the 13.____

    A. salaries paid to the employees
    B. amounts paid to independent contractors for services rendered
    C. amounts taken by the proprietor for his personal use
    D. total of payments made for general expenses of the business

14. The phrase *2%/10 net 30 days* on an invoice ORDINARILY means that 14.____

    A. 2% of the amount must be paid within 30 days
    B. the purchaser must add 2% to the amount of the invoice if he fails to pay within 30 days
    C. the entire amount must be paid within 30 days
    D. the purchaser may deduct 2% from the amount if he pays within 30 days

15. The ESSENTIAL characteristic of a C.O.D. sale of merchandise is that the 15.____

    A. purchaser pays for the merchandise upon its receipt by him
    B. seller guarantees the merchandise to be as specified by him
    C. merchandise is delivered by a common carrier
    D. purchaser is permitted to pay for the merchandise in convenient installments

16. If the drawer of a check makes an error in writing the amount of the check, he should   16._____

    A. erase the error and insert the correct amount
    B. cross out the error and insert the correct amount
    C. destroy the check and prepare another one
    D. write the correct amount directly above the incorrect one

17. States do NOT levy a(n) _____ tax.   17._____

    A. unemployment insurance   B. income
    C. corporation franchise   D. export

18. The cost of goods sold by a retail store is PROPERLY determined by   18._____

    A. *adding* the closing inventory to the total of the opening inventory and the purchases for the year
    B. *deducting* the closing inventory from the total of the opening inventory and the purchases for the year
    C. *deducting* the total of the opening and closing inventories from the purchases for the year
    D. *adding* the total of the opening and closing inventories

19. The PRIMARY purpose of a trial balance is to determine   19._____

    A. that all transactions have been entered in the journals
    B. the accuracy of the totals in the general ledger
    C. the correctness of the amounts entered in the journals
    D. that amounts have been posted to the proper accounts in the general ledger

20. The SURPLUS account of a corporation is *ordinarily* used to record   20._____

    A. the actual amount subscribed by stockholders
    B. the amount of profits earned by the corporation
    C. any excess of current assets over current liabilities
    D. the total of the fixed assets of the corporation

Questions 21-30.

DIRECTIONS: Each of Questions 21 to 30 consists of a typical transaction of Our Business followed by the debit and credit (amounts omitted) of the journal entry for that transaction. For each of these questions, the debit and credit given may be appropriately classified under one of the following categories:

    A. The debit of the journal entry is CORRECT but the credit is INCORRECT.
    B. The debit of the journal entry is INCORRECT but the credit is CORRECT.
    C. BOTH the debit and the credit of the journal entry are correct.
    D. BOTH the debit and the credit of the journal entry are incorrect.

Examine each question carefully. Then, in the correspondingly numbered space on the right, mark as your answer the letter preceding the category which is the BEST of the four suggested above.

SAMPLE QUESTION: We purchased a desk for cash.
                              Debit: Office Equipment
                              Credit: Accounts Payable

In this example, the debit is correct but the credit is incorrect. Therefore, you should mark A as your answer.

21. We sent a check for $500 to F. Thomas in payment for an invoice for that amount.   21._____
     Debit: Cash   Credit: Accounts Receivable

22. We took merchandise, amounting to $35, for our own use.   22._____
     Debit: Proprietor, Personal   Credit: Purchases

23. Arthur Townsend's 90-day note for $350, which was discounted by us at our bank last   23._____
     month, was paid by him today.
     Debit: Notes Receivable Discounted
     Credit: Accounts Receivable

24. We sold merchandise to T. Wilson on account of $275.   24._____
     Debit: Accounts Payable   Credit: Sales

25. We returned damaged merchandise to B. Lowell and received a credit memorandum   25._____
     from him for $28.
     Debit: Accounts Payable
     Credit: Sales Returns and Allowances

26. We paid our 30-day note given to Mr. Kane for $650 without interest.   26._____
     Debit: Notes Receivable   Credit: Cash

27. We sent Chet Carr a check for $10.50 for a discount he had forgotten to take when he   27._____
     paid us for merchandise this week.
     Debit: Sales Discounts   Credit: Cash

28. The bank loaned us $1000, and we invested it in the business.   28._____
     Debit: Cash   Credit: Loan Receivable

29. We recorded depreciation for the year on our office equipment.   29._____
     Debit: Reserve for Depreciation of Office Equipment
     Credit: Depreciation of Office Equipment

30. One of our customers, Allen Koren, was declared bankrupt and his debt of $25 to us was   30._____
     canceled.
     Debit: Reserve for Bad Debts Credit: Accounts Receivable

Questions 31-45.

DIRECTIONS: Questions 31 to 45 consist of a list of some of the accounts in the general led-
                      ger of a corporation which operates a retail store. Indicate whether each
                      account listed contains generally a debit or credit balance by marking the letter
                      D (for debit balance) or the letter C (for credit balance) in the correspondingly
                      numbered space on the right.
                      For example, for the account Cash, which generally contains a debit balance,
                      you would mark the letter D as your answer.

31. Rent Expense   31.____

32. Allowance for Depreciation of Fixtures   32.____

33. Sales Returns and Allowances   33.____

34. Security Deposit for Electricity   34.____

35. Accrued Salaries Payable   35.____

36. Dividends Payable   36.____

37. Petty Cash Fund   37.____

38. Notes Receivable Discounted   38.____

39. Surplus   39.____

40. Capital Stock Authorized   40.____

41. Insurance Expense   41.____

42. Sales for Cash   42.____

43. Purchase Discounts   43.____

44. Automobile Delivery Equipment   44.____

45. Bad Debts Expense   45.____

Questions 46-60.

DIRECTIONS: Questions 46 to 60 consist of a list of some of the accounts in a general ledger. For the purpose of preparing financial statements, each of these accounts is to be classified into one of the following five major classifications, lettered A to E, as follows:
A. Assets   B. Liabilities   C. Income   D. Expense   E. Capital You are to indicate the classification to which each belongs by marking the appropriate letter, A, B, C, D or E. in the correspondingly numbered space on the right. For example, for the account MERCHANDISE INVENTORY, which is an asset account, you would mark the letter A as your answer.

46. Purchases   46.____

47. Prepaid Interest   47.____

48. Cash in Bank   48.____

49. Depreciation of Fixtures   49.____

50. Accounts Receivable 50.____

51. Mortgage Payable 51.____

52. Accrued Interest Receivable 52.____

53. Bad Debts 53.____

54. Insurance Expired 54.____

55. Treasury Stock 55.____

56. Investments 56.____

57. Loan to Partner 57.____

58. Unearned Rent Received 58.____

59. Petty Cash Fund 59.____

60. Loss on Sale of Equipment 60.____

KEY (CORRECT ANSWERS)

1.	B	16.	C	31.	D	46.	D
2.	A	17.	D	32.	C	47.	A
3.	D	18.	B	33.	D	48.	A
4.	A	19.	B	34.	D	49.	D
5.	C	20.	B	35.	C	50.	A
6.	B	21.	D	36.	C	51.	B
7.	A	22.	C	37.	D	52.	A
8.	D	23.	A	38.	C	53.	D
9.	D	24.	B	39.	C	54.	D
10.	C	25.	A	40.	C	55.	E
11.	D	26.	B	41.	D	56.	A
12.	B	27.	C	42.	C	57.	A
13.	C	28.	A	43.	C	58.	B
14.	C	29.	D	44.	D	59.	A
15.	A	30.	C	45.	D	60.	D

EXAMINATION SECTION

TEST 1

DIRECTIONS: Each question or incomplete statement is followed by several suggested answers or completions Select the one that BEST answers the question or completes the statement. *PRINT THE LETTER OF THE CORRECT ANSWER IN THE SPACE AT THE RIGHT.*

Questions 1-25.

DIRECTIONS: Below you will find the Cash Receipts Journal of John Walker, a merchant. Under the heading of each money column of the Journals, there is a letter of the alphabet. Following the Journals there is a series of transactions. You are to determine the entry for each transaction and then show in the space at the right the columns to be used.

    For example: If a certain transaction entered in the Cash Receipts Journal results in an entry of $100 in the General Ledger Column and $100 in the Net Cash Column, in the appropriate space at the right you should write: A,E. If the record of the transaction requires the use of more than two columns, your answer should contain more than two letters.

    Do not put the amounts in your answer space. The letters of the columns in the Cash Journals to be used are sufficient.

    If a transaction requires no entry in the Cash Journals, write "None" in the appropriate space at the right, even though a record would be made in some other journal.

CASH RECEIPTS JOURNAL

Date	Account Credited	Explanation	F	General Ledger	Accts. Rec.	Cash Sales	Disc. on Sales	Net Cash
				A	B	C	D	E

CASH PAYMENTS JOURNAL

Date	Acct. Debited	Explanation	F	General Ledger	Accts. Pay.	Soc. Sec. Taxes Pay.	With. Taxes Pay.	Disc. on Purch.	Net Cash
				F	G	H	I	J	K

1. Cash Sales amounted to $280.

    1._____

2. Paid employees' salaries for the week. The check amounted to $346 after deducting $4.00 for Social Security Taxes and $30 for Income Taxes withheld.

    2._____

3. A check received in the mail from R. Walters was in payment of a bill of $150, terms 2/10, n/30. The customer had taken the discount.

    3._____

4. The proprietor, Mr. Walker, took merchandise valued at $30 from the stockroom for his personal use.

4._____

5. Prepaid $15 freight on shipment of goods to H. Lane, a customer, and charged his account.

5._____

6. Sent a check for $250 to P. Packer to apply on account.

6._____

7. Drew a check for $75 to start a Petty Cash fund.

7._____

8. H. Wall sent us a check for $700 in payment of his 60-day note for $700. The note was interest bearing (6%), but he failed to pay us the interest. We deposited the $700 check and wrote to him requesting an additional check.

8._____

9. Paid rent for month $180.

9._____

10. Received a check for $70 from K. London to apply on account.

10._____

11. H. Wall sent us a check for the interest due on note (see Item 8).

11._____

12. Paid our 30-day note for $460 due today which we had given to G. Thompson.

12._____

13. Accepted a trade acceptance drawn by R. Sparks on us for invoice of $722.

13._____

14. Borrowed at our bank on our $1,500 note. Net proceeds, $1,485. (The bookkeeper used only one journal to make a complete and correct entry. You are to do likewise.)

14._____

15. Received a check for $60 from W. Saks, a creditor, refunding our overpayment to him on our account.

15._____

16. A check from H. Low, which was deposited by us last month, was returned to us marked "insufficient funds." The check amounted to $55 and had been sent to us to settle his account.

16._____

17. Drew a sight draft on R. Coe for overdue account of $120. Left draft at bank for collection.

17._____

18. Paid $26 freight on goods purchased from W. Lincoln of Chicago, terms f.o.b. Chicago.

18._____

19. Mailed a credit memorandum to E. Stern for return of defective merchandise sold him on account for $65.

19._____

20. The proprietor, John Walker, drew $90 cash for personal use.

20._____

21. Received a money order for $110 from B. Kiner for invoice of merchandise charged to him.

21._____

22. Mr. Walker, proprietor, drew $1,200 from his personal savings account and invested the entire sum in his business.   22.____

23. Issued check to Clark & Co. in payment of invoice amounting to $500. Discount of 3% was taken.   23.____

24. Received a 30-day non-interest bearing note for $610 from A. Allen for merchandise sold him today.   24.____

25. Sent a check for $51 to Collector of Internal Revenue for Social Security Taxes collected for the past three months.   25.____

Questions 26-35.

DIRECTIONS: Below you will find the General Journal used by D. Prince, wholesaler. Under the heading of each money column you will find a letter of the alphabet. Following the General Journal, there is a series of transactions. You are to determine the correct entry for each transaction and then show in the appropriate space at the right the columns to be used.

For example: If a certain transaction results in an entry of $100 in the Notes Receivable Column (on the left side) and an entry of $100 in the General Ledger Column (on the right side), in the appropriate space at the right you should write A, D.

If the record of the transaction requires the use of more than two columns, your answer should contain more than two letters.

Do not put the amounts on your answer space. The letters of the columns to be used are sufficient.

If a transaction requires no entry in the General Journal, write "None" in the appropriate space at the right, even though a record would be made in some other journal.

GENERAL JOURNAL

Notes Rec.	Accts. Pay.	General Ledger	L. F.		General Ledger	Accts. Rec.	Notes Payable
A	B	C			D	E	F

26. Issued a credit memorandum for $58 to J. Winston for goods returned to us.   26.____

27. P. Jones sent us his 60-day note for $750 in full settlement of his account.   27.____

28. Sent a 60-day note to J. O'Connor for invoice of $375 less 2%.   28.____

29. H. Owens sent us a credit memorandum for overcharge of $75 on invoice.   29.____

30. Mailed a 30-day draft to W. Kinder, a customer, for his acceptance amounting to $375 for invoice of goods sold him yesterday.   30.____

31. A. Hocker, a customer, went out of business owing us $170. The claim is considered worthless.
31._____

32. The proprietor requested the bookkeeper to provide a reserve of $500 for expected losses on customers' accounts.
32._____

33. P. Winston sent us a $350 bank draft in full settlement of his account.
33._____

34. Accepted a 30-day trade acceptance drawn by A. Hall for bill of goods amounting to $316 purchased by us last week.
34._____

35. Mr. D. Prince, the proprietor, takes his brother, L. Prince, into the business as an equal partner. Mr. L. Prince invests merchandise worth $3,500 in the business and becomes a partner.
35._____

Questions 36-50.

DIRECTIONS: Below you will find a list of accounts from the ledger of R. Lincoln. There is a letter of the alphabet before each account.

Using the letter in front of each account title (using no accounts not listed), make journal entries for the transactions given below.

Do not write the names of the accounts in your answer space. Simply indicate in the proper space at the right the letters of the accounts to be debited or credited.

Always give the letter or letters of accounts to be debited first, then give the letter or letters of accounts to be credited.

For example, if Office Supplies and Delivery Expenses are to be debited and Notes Payable and Cash are to be credited in a certain transaction, then write as your answer L, D; K, C.

A.	Accounts Payable	J.	Notes Receivable Discounted
B.	Accounts Receivable	K.	Notes Payable
C.	Cash	L.	Office Supplies
D.	Delivery Expense	M.	R. Lincoln, Personal
E.	Discount on Purchases	N.	Petty Cash
F.	Freight Inward	O.	Purchase Returns
G.	Interest Cost	P.	Sales Discount
H.	Purchases	R.	Sales Returns
I.	Notes Receivable	S.	Sales Income

36. Paid the Fox Transportation Co. $15 by check for express charges on goods delivered to us.
36._____

37. Accepted a 30-day trade acceptance for $850 drawn on us by Allen & Co.
37._____

38. Returned damaged goods to H. Parker and he sent us a credit memorandum for $47.
38._____

39. John Smith's 30-day note for $800, which was discounted by us at our bank last month, was paid by him today.

39.____

40. Paid our 60-day note due today in favor of S. Paul for $600 with interest. The check amounted to $606.

40.____

41. The total of the Notes Payable column in the General Journal amounted to $450 at the end of last month. It was posted in error to the Notes Receivable Discounted account. Make the correction entry.

41.____

42. Issued a check to J. News in settlement of invoice $500 less 2%.

42.____

43. Paid Stern Stationers $5.00 by check for four reams of paper for office use.

43.____

44. Sent a check for $48 to Gregory's Garage for storage, gasoline, oil, and service on auto trucks.

44.____

45. Drew a check for $100 to establish a Petty Cash fund.

45.____

46. A. Black, a customer, settled his account of $400 by sending us a check for $100 and a 30-day note for the balance.

46.____

47. J. Walters failed to deduct a discount of $10 when he paid us last month. He called the matter to our attention and we sent him a check for $10.

47.____

48. Donated to the Salvation Army merchandise out of stock costing the proprietor $75.

48.____

49. At the end of the year, the Sales Returns account had a balance of $225. make the entry to close this account.

49.____

50. At the end of the year, the Freight Inward account had a balance of $450. Make the entry to close this account.

50.____

Questions 51-60.

DIRECTIONS: In answering Questions 51 through 60, print the CORRECT answer in the space at the right.

51. On December 31, a bookkeeper prepared a Profit and Loss Statement in which the following are some of the items listed:

Sales	$50,000
Purchases	45,000
Inventory (Jan. 1)	7,500
Sales Returns	400
Gross Profit	15,000
Selling expense	3,200

Find the Inventory of Merchandise on December 31.

51.____

52. A. Landers invested $5,000 in cash in a new business. At the end of the
year, he finds he has $2,500 in cash, $1,000 in furniture, $1,800 in
merchandise on which he owes $750. During the year, Mr. Landers drew
$2,400 for his own use. What was his profit or loss for the year? (Write P or L
before the figure.)

52.____

53. Wm. Abbott purchased a machine for $2,800. The estimated life of the
machine was five years. At the end of five years, the machine could be sold for
scrap for $400. Find the depreciation charge at the end of the first six months
of use.

53.____

54. On January 1, A. Menton's Capital was $2,400. His partner, P. King, had
a Capital of $6,000. Their agreement provided for dividing profits in proportion
to Capital. During the year the Net Profit was $12,480. What was A. Menton's
share of the Net Profit?

54.____

55. On December 31, J. Klein's ledger, after all closing entries, contained the
following balances:

Cash	$5,000
Merchandise Inventory	1,500
Accounts Receivable	8,000
Notes Receivable	2,000
Deferred Expense	300
Furniture and Fixtures	1,200
Accounts Payable	4,000
Reserve for Bad Debts	600
Notes Receivable Discounted	800
Reserve for Depreciation of Furniture and Fixtures	900

What was J. Klein's Capital on December 31?

55.____

56. An employer paid $160 in Social Security taxes at the rate of 1% on taxable
wages. He expects to employ more persons next year and pay out 50% more
in taxable wages than he did. What will be his Social Security costs at the new
rate of 1½% next year?

56.____

57. On June 17, you discounted a customer's 60-day note at your bank. The
face of the note was $840 and it was dated June 5, discount rate 6%. What
was the amount of the net proceeds?

57.____

58. On June 18, you sold I. Cohen, of Chicago, merchandise. The invoice
totaled $684, which included $38 freight which you had prepaid. Terms were 2,
10, n/30, f.o.b. New York. If Mr. Cohen pays you on June 27, what should be
the CORRECT amount of the check?

58.____

59. A bankrupt firm agrees to pay its creditors 30 cents on the dollar. It pays
Klein & Co. $12,600. What was Klein & Co.'s loss?

59.____

60. A salesman earned $15,600 in one year. His commissions were at the rate of 7½% of sales. What were his sales for the year?   60.____

Questions 61-80.

DIRECTIONS: Questions 61 through 80 are to be answered on the basis of the following:

The bookkeeper of Walters Co. began to make a trial balance of his General Ledger on December 31. Before he had completed his trial balance, you were permitted to examine his work.

If a balance is in the correct column, print "C" in the appropriate space at the right. If a balance is in the wrong column, print "W" in the appropriate space at the right.

Caution: Since the trial balance is not complete, do not attempt to strike a balance of the figures given in the question.

WALTER CO.
Trial Balance, December 31

61.	Merchandise, Inventory, Jan. 1	16,000		61.____
62.	Freight Inward	150		62.____
63.	Petty Cash		75	63.____
64.	Interest Income	70		64.____
65.	Notes Receivable	4,000		65.____
66.	Sales		17,000	66.____
67.	Sales Discount		170	67.____
68.	Purchase Returns	250		68.____
69.	Auto Trucks	9,000		69.____
70.	Reserve for Depreciation of Furniture	770		70.____
71.	Bad Debts		160	71.____
72.	Sales Taxes Collected	225		72.____
73.	Sales Returns		485	73.____
74.	Reserve for Bad Debts		500	74.____
75.	Deposits with Landlord		150	75.____

76.	Accrued Interest on Notes Receivable	50	76._____
77.	Income from Commissions	900	77._____
78.	Purchase Discounts	110	78._____
79.	Depreciation of Furniture	225	79._____
80.	Notes and Acceptances from Customers	780	80._____

KEY (CORRECT ANSWERS)

1.	C, E	21.	B, E	41.	J; K	61.	C
2.	F, H, I, K	22.	A, E	42.	A; C, E	62.	C
3.	B, D, E	23.	G, J, K	43.	L; C	63.	W
4.	None	24.	None	44.	D; C	64.	W
5.	F, K	25.	F, K	45.	N; C	65.	C
6.	G, K	26.	C, E	46.	I, C; B	66.	C
7.	F, K	27.	A, E	47.	P; C	67.	W
8.	A, E	28.	B, D, F	48.	M; H	68.	W
9.	F, K	29.	B, D	49.	H; F	69.	C
10.	B, E	30.	None	50.	H; F	70.	W
11.	A, E	31.	C, E	51.	17900	71.	W
12.	F, K	32.	C, D	52.	P1950	72.	W
13.	None	33.	None	53.	220	73.	W
14.	A, D, E	34.	B, F	54.	3565.71	74.	C
15.	A, E	35.	C, D	55.	11700	75.	W
16.	F, K	36.	F; C	56.	360	76.	W
17.	None	37.	A; K	57.	833.28	77.	C
18.	F, K	38.	A; O	58.	671.08	78.	C
19.	None	39.	J; K	59.	29400	79.	W
20.	F, K	40.	K, G; C	60.	208000	80.	W

TEST 2

DIRECTIONS: Each question or incomplete statement is followed by several suggested answers or completions. Select the one that BEST answers the question or completes the statement. *PRINT THE LETTER OF THE CORRECT ANSWER IN THE SPACE AT THE RIGHT.*

Questions 1-25.

DIRECTIONS: Below you will find:
1. General Ledger balances on January 31, appearing in books of A. New.
2. All entries on books of A. New for month of February
3. You are to supply balances of ledger accounts on February 29, in the appropriate spaces at the right, as indicated at the end of these questions.

The correct balances in A. New's General Ledger on January 31 were as follows: Cash $7,642; Notes Receivable $2,600; Accounts Receivable $3,100; Furniture and Fixtures $750; Delivery Equipment $1,200; Purchases $2,850; Telephone and Telegrams $110; Office Supplies $380; Salaries $300; Sales Discount $80; Purchase Discount $56; Insurance $160; Sales $3,150; Freight Inward $70; Accounts Payable $2,400; Freight Outward (debit) $40; Notes Payable $1,100; A. New Capital $12,200; A. New Personal (credit) $310; Sales Taxes Payable $35; Withholding Taxes Payable $28; and Social Security Taxes Payable $3.

CASH RECEIPTS

Date	Name	Net Cash	Sales Disc.	Accts. Rec.	Miscellaneous Account	Amount
2/2	S. Wilson	471.00	9.00	480.00		
2/5	First Nat'l Bank	500.00			Notes Pay.	500.00
2/16	M. Tower	350.00			Notes Rec.	340.00
					Int. Income	10.00
2/20	Paul Smith	245.00	5.00	250.00		
2/28	Sundry Customers	110.00			Sales	110.00
	TOTALS	$1675.00	$14.00	$730.00		$960.00

CASH DISBURSEMENTS

Date	Name	Net Cash	Purch. Disc.	Soc. Sec. Tax	With-hold. Taxes	Accts. Pay.	Miscellaneous Account	Amount
2/3	Sun Realty Co.	125					Rent	125
2/9	Bell Smith Co.	540	10			550		
2/10	First Nat'l Bank	808					Notes Pay.	800
							Int. Cost	8
2/14	James Roe Co.	1360	22			1382		
2/16	Roxy Desk Co.	125					Fur. & Fixt.	125
2/20	Baldwin Auto	1650					Del. & Equip.	1650
2/28	Payroll	360		4	36		Sal.	400
2/28	A. New	215					A. New Pers.	215
	TOTALS	$5183	32	4	36	1932		3323

SALES BOOK

Date	Name	Accts. Rec.	Sales	Freight Out	Sales Tax
2/2	Booth &White	460.00	455.00	5.00	
2/10	Water & Co.	375.00	364.00	11.00	
2/14	Neville Bros.	204.00	200.00		4.00
2/16	A. Parker	918.00	900.00		18.00
	TOTALS	$1957.00	1919.00	16.00	22.00

PURCHASE BOOK

Date	Name	Accts. Payable	Purchases	Freight Inward	Miscellaneous Account	Amount
2/4	Walden Co.	800.00	800.00			
2/5	Power Telephone	17.00			Tel.	17.00
2/9	Mfgs. Ins. Co.	122.00			Insurance	122.00
2/12	Tower & Co.	756.00	748.00	8.00		
2/16	X-cel Express	13.00		13.00		
2/23	Braver & Co.	265.00	265.00			
2/28	Penn Stationers	65.00			Off. Suppl.	65.00
	TOTALS	$2038.00	1813.00	21.00		204.00

Supply the balances of the following accounts on February 29, after all posting has been done for February. Print the answers in the appropriate spaces at the right. (Give amounts only.)

1. Cash   1.____

2. Notes Receivable   2.____

3. Accounts Receivable   3.____

4. Furniture and Fixtures   4.____

5. Delivery Equipment   5.____

6. Purchases   6.____

7. Telephone   7.____

8. Office Supplies   8.____

9. Salaries   9.____

10. Sales Discount   10.____

11. Purchase Discount   11.____

12. Insurance   12.____

13. Freight Inward   13.____

14. Sales   14.____

15. Accounts Payable   15.____

16. Freight Outward   16.____

17. Notes Payable   17.____

18. A. New, Capital   18.____

19. A. New, Personal   19.____

20. Sales Taxes Payable   20.____

21. Withholding Taxes Payable   21.____

22. Social Security Taxes Payable   22.____

23. Interest Income   23.____

24. Rent   24.____

25. Interest Cost   25.____

Questions 26-50.

DIRECTIONS: Below is a list of some of the accounts containing balances in the ledger of the
Ajax Company on December 31st after posting all entries for the year, except
adjusting and closing entries.
    If the account normally would have a debit balance, write "D" in the proper
numbered space at the right. If the amount normally would have a credit
balance, write "C" in the proper numbered space at the right.

26. Notes Receivable   26.____

27. Merchandise Inventory   27.____

28. Notes Payable   28.____

29. Interest on Notes Receivable   29.____

30. Freight Inward   30.____

31. Sales Discount   31.____

32. Samuel Ajax Proprietor   32.____

33. Purchase Returns and Allowances   33.____

34. Land and Buildings   34.____

35. Reserve for Depreciation of Furniture and Fixtures   35.____

36. Purchase Discount   36.____

37. Rent Collected from Sub-Tenants   37.____

38. Taxes Accrued   38.____

39. Notes Receivable Discounted   39.____

40. Accounts Payable   40.____

41. Interest on Notes Payable   41.____

42. Sales Returns and Allowances   42.____

43. Reserve for Bad Debts   43.____

44. Income from Commissions   44.____

45. Deposits from Customers on Containers   45.____

46. Sales   46.____

47. Accounts Receivable   47.____

48. United States Government Bonds   48.____

49. Sales Taxes Collected   49.____

50. Deposit with Gas Company   50.____

Questions 51-90.

DIRECTIONS: As an employee for Wallace and Pace, you have taken a trial balance of the
General Ledger on December 31. After posting all adjusting entries but before
closing the accounts, you find your adjusted trial balance is correct. You are
now requested to prepare a classified balance sheet using only the following
classifications:
    A. Current Assets
    B. Fixed Assets
    C. Deferred Charges
    D. Current Liabilities
    E. Fixed Liabilities
    F. Capital

5 (#2)

Indicate the balance sheet classification of the following items by putting the letter (A to F) in the corresponding spaces at the right. However, if any of the following items should *not* appear in our classified balance sheet, write the letter "P" in the corresponding space at the right.

51. Cash   51._____

52. Furniture and Fixtures   52._____

53. Notes Receivable   53._____

54. Reserve for Bad Debts   54._____

55. Merchandise Inventory 1/1   55._____

56. Freight In   56._____

57. A. Wallace, Capital   57._____

58. Sales Returns   58._____

59. Notes Payable   59._____

60. Purchase Discount   60._____

61. Reserve for Depreciation of Furniture and Fixtures   61._____

62. Insurance Unexpired   62._____

63. Interest Cost   63._____

64. Salaries   64._____

65. Shipping Supplies Inventory as of 12/31   65._____

66. Accounts Receivable   66._____

67. Bad Debts   67._____

68. Shipping Supplies   68._____

69. Mortgage Payable   69._____

70. Depreciation on Furniture and Fixtures   70._____

71. L. Pace, Personal (credit)   71._____

72. Land, Buildings   72._____

73. Depreciation on Buildings   73.____

74. Interest Accrued on Notes Receivable   74.____

75. Petty Cash Fund   75.____

76. Taxes   76.____

77. Sales Discount   77.____

78. Merchandise Inventory 12/31   78.____

79. Sales   79.____

80. Interest Income   80.____

81. Purchases   81.____

82. Insurance   82.____

83. Accounts Payable   83.____

84. Salaries Accrued   84.____

85. Reserve for Depreciation of Buildings   85.____

86. Taxes Payable   86.____

87. Purchase Returns   87.____

88. Interest Accrued on Mortgage   88.____

89. A. Wallace, Personal (debit)   89.____

90. L. Pace, Capital   90.____

Questions 91-110.

DIRECTIONS: Below you will find a list of accounts with a number before each:

1. Accounts Payable	11. Petty Cash Fund
2. Accounts Receivable	12. Proprietor's Capital Account
3. Cash	13. Purchases
4. Freight Inward	14. Purchase Discounts
5. Freight Outward	15. Purchase Returns
6. Interest Cost	16. Real Estate
7. Interest Income	17. Sales
8. Notes Payable	18. Sales Discounts
9. Notes Receivable	19. Selling Expenses
10. Notes Receivable Discounted	20. Selling Expenses

Using the number in front of each account, make journal entries for the transactions listed below.

Do not write the names of the accounts in your answer space. Simply indicate in the proper space at the right the numbers of the accounts to be debited or credited. Always give the number of the account to be debited first, then give the number of the account to be credited.

Example: If Cash is to be debited and Sales is to be credited, write as your answer 3-17.

91. Drew a check to establish a Petty Cash Fund.   91.____

92. A. Paul, a customer, sent us a 60-day interest-bearing note for an invoice previously entered on our books.   92.____

93. Sent a credit memorandum to a customer for goods returned to us.   93.____

94. Our bank notified us that a customer's check was returned marked "insufficient funds."   94.____

95. Accepted a 60-day draft drawn on us by a creditor for invoice previously entered on the books.   95.____

96. A customer sent us a check as a deposit on goods to be sent him.   96.____

97. Issued a certified check for the purchase of real estate.   97.____

98. Received notice from the bank that our account was charged for the payment of trade acceptance given to a creditor two months ago.   98.____

99. Returned merchandise to a creditor and received a credit memorandum.   99.____

100. Sent a check to a customer whose account had been overpaid in error.   100.____

101. The proprietor invested additional cash in the business.   101.____

102. Received a bank draft from a customer in payment of a note.   102.____

103. Sent our 90-day interest-bearing note to a creditor in settlement of account.   103.____

104. Honored a sight draft drawn on us by one of our creditors.   104.____

105. Sold goods to a customer, terms 60 days.   105.____

106. A customer's note, which we had discounted two months ago, was collected by our bank.   106.____

107. Purchased merchandise, terms 2/10 E.O.M.   107.____

108. Paid our note today.   108._____

109. A customer notifies us that he failed to deduct a discount on his last   109._____
remittance. Sent him a check for the discount.

110. Last month's total of the Accounts Receivable column in the Cash Receipts   110._____
book was posted in error to Notes Receivable Account. Make the correction
entry.

Questions 111-112

DIRECTIONS: Questions 111 and 112 are to be answered based on the following:

T. Lawson uses controlling accounts and a card system for the individual accounts with his
customers and creditors.
The card containing the account with G. White, to whom he sells goods, has been lost.
Reference to monthly schedules of Accounts Receivable shows that White owed $3500 on April
1; $2900 on May 1; and $4300 on June 1.
The cash book shows that Lawson received the following payments from White: $2500 on
April 7; $3400 on April 14; and $3800 on May 25.
The journal shows that damaged goods were returned by White on April 15, $250, and
that White received an allowance of $50 for shortages on May 16. White gave Lawson a note
for $3200 on May 30.

111. What were the Sales to White during April?   111._____

112. What were the Sales to White during May?   112._____

Questions 113-114

DIRECTIONS: Questions 113 and 114 are to be answered on the basis of the following:

Your cash book balance on July 31 was $9242.18.
The bank statement sent to you on August 1 shows a credit for interest of $16.20 and a
deduction of $4.50 for collection expenses.
You discover that one check paid by the bank was made out for $78.29 and you had
entered it in the cash book as $72.89.
The checks outstanding are #235 for $409.08; #240 for $279; #241 for $42.10; and #247
for $913.56.

113. What balance did the bank report?   113._____

114. What was your true cash balance on August 1?   114._____

115. You received an invoice dated Sept. 5, terms 2/10, n/30, f.o.b. destination,   115._____
amounting to $350. The shipper paid $25 freight. On Sept. 8 you received a
credit memorandum for $15 worth of goods returned. What was the amount of
the check required to pay the invoice on Sept. 14?

116. On March 3 you drew a check to pay an invoice of $750, terms 2/10, E.O.M., dated Feb. 3. What was the amount of the check?

116.____

117. On March 14 you drew a check to pay an invoice of $460, which included $30 freight prepaid by shipper. Invoice dated March 6 carried items 5/10, n/60. What was the amount of the check?

117.____

118. March 15 – Your employer borrowed from his bank on his own 90-day note for $1400. Rate of discount 6%. What amount should you enter in your net cash column in your cash receipts book?

118.____

119. May 9 – You discounted a customer's 60-day note at your bank. Face of note was $480. Date of note was May 3rd. Discount rate was 6%. What was the amount of the net proceeds?

119.____

120. Your Dec. 31 trial balance contained an item for Interest Income $165. On that date you discovered that you had collected $15 interest in advance, and that there was $22 interest accrued on customers' notes not yet due. What amount should be listed on the year's Profit and Loss Statement as interest income?

120.____

KEY (CORRECT ANSWERS)

1.	4135	26.	D	51.	A	76.	P	101.	3-12
2.	2260	27.	D	52.	B	77.	P	102.	3-9
3.	4327	28.	C	53.	A	78.	A	103.	1-8
4.	875	29.	C	54.	A	79.	P	104.	1-3
5.	2850	30.	D	55.	P	80.	P	105.	2-17
6.	4663	31.	D	56.	P	81.	P	106.	10-9
7.	127	32.	C	57.	F	82.	P	107.	13-1
8.	445	33.	C	58.	P	83.	D	108.	8-3
9.	700	34.	D	59.	D	84.	D	109.	18-3
10.	94	35.	C	60.	P	85.	B	110.	9-2
11.	88	36.	C	61.	B	86.	D	111.	5550
12.	282	37.	C	62.	A	87.	P	112.	8450
13.	91	38.	C	63.	P	88.	D	113.	10892.41
14.	5179	39.	C	64.	P	89.	F	114.	9248.48
15.	2506	40.	C	65.	A	90.	F	115.	328.30
16.	24	41.	D	66.	A	91.	11-3	116.	735
17.	800	42.	D	67.	P	92.	9-2	117.	438.50
18.	12200	43.	C	68.	P	93.	19-2	118.	1379
19.	95	44.	C	69.	E	94.	2-3	119.	475.68
20.	57	45.	C	70.	P	95.	1-8	120.	172
21.	64	46.	C	71.	F	96.	3-2		
22.	7	47.	D	72.	B	97.	16-3		
23.	10	48.	D	73.	P	98.	8-3		
24.	125	49.	C	74.	A	99.	1-15		
25.	8	50.	D	75.	A	100.	2-3		

___

EXAMINATION SECTION

TEST 1

DIRECTIONS: Each question or incomplete statement is followed by several suggested answers or completions. Select the one that BEST answers the question or completes the statement. *PRINT THE LETTER OF THE CORRECT ANSWER IN THE SPACE AT THE RIGHT.*

Questions 1-20.

DIRECTIONS: Listed below in T accounts are the five MAJOR classifications of accounts. Consider carefully each of the following statements and indicate the change by writing the appropriate letter from the T accounts in the space at the right.

ASSETS	LIABILITIES	PROPRIETORSHIP	INCOME	EXPENSES
A | B	C | D	E | F	G | H	I | J

Sample Question:
A decrease in cash
The CORRECT answer is B.

1. An increase in equipment

1.____

2. An increase in the proprietorship

2.____

3. An increase in office salaries

3.____

4. A decrease in accounts payable

4.____

5. An increase in merchandise inventory

5.____

6. A decrease in office equipment

6.____

7. A decrease in office supplies

7.____

8. An increase in the proprietor's drawing account

8.____

9. A withdrawal of capital by the proprietor

9.____

10. An increase in sales

10.____

11. An increase in salaries payable

11.____

12. An increase in the net profit for the period

12.____

13. An increase in the sales returns and allowances

13.____

14. A decrease in purchases   14._____

15. A decrease in the accounts receivable   15._____

16. An increase in the mortgage payable   16._____

17. An increase in delivery expense   17._____

18. An increase in notes payable   18._____

19. An increase in purchases returns and allowances   19._____

20. A decrease in delivery equipment   20._____

Questions 21-40.

DIRECTIONS: Indicate the title of the accounts to be debited and credited in journalizing, adjusting, and closing the transactions given below by writing in the space at the right the letters that correspond to the accounts listed at the right.

Sample Question:
Paid the rent for the month, $100   Debit   Credit
                                                             K   C

				Debit	Credit
21.	C.M. Smith invested $10,000 in the	A.	Accounts Payable	21._____	_____
	business	B.	Accounts Receivable		
		C.	Cash		
22.	Purchased merchandise on	D.	Income & Expense	22._____	_____
	account from A.D. Hall, $875		Summary		
		E.	Insurance		
23.	Sold merchandise on account to	F.	Insurance Expense	23._____	_____
	L.S. Brook, $500	G.	Merchandise		
			Inventory		
24.	Received $250 from cash sales	H.	Office Supplies	24._____	_____
		I.	Office Supplies		
25.	Purchased office supplies for		Used	25._____	_____
	cash, $90	J.	Purchases		
		K.	Rent Expense		
26.	Paid A.D. Hall $500 to apply	L.	Salaries	26._____	_____
	on account	M.	Salaries Payable		
		N.	Sales		
27.	Paid insurance premium for the	O.	C.M. Smith, Capital	27._____	_____
	year, $360	P.	C.M. Smith, Drawing		
28.	Paid C.M. Smith $100 for personal			28._____	_____
	use				
29.	Received $300 from L.S. Brooks,			29._____	_____
	to apply on account				

30. Paid salaries for the month $500

30.____ ____

Adjusting Entries

31. The supplies used during the month
were $60

31.____ ____

32. The salaries owed at the close of
the month were $40

32.____ ____

33. The prepaid insurance expired was $30

33.____ ____

34. The beginning merchandise inventory
was $1200

34.____ ____

35. The closing merchandise inventory
was $750

35.____ ____

Closing Entries

36. The sales account has a balance
of $4500

36.____ ____

37. The salaries for the month were $540

37.____ ____

38. The purchase account balance is $3600

38.____ ____

39. The office supplies used were $75

39.____ ____

40. The income and expense summary has
a net profit of $350

40.____ ____

KEY (CORRECT ANSWERS)

						DEBIT	CREDIT			DEBIT	CREDIT
1.	A		11.	D	21.	C	O	31.	I	H
2.	F		12.	F	22.	J	A	32.	L	M
3.	I		13.	G	23.	B	N	33.	F	E
4.	C		14.	J	24.	C	N	34.	D	G
5.	A		15.	B	25.	H	C	35.	G	D
6.	B		16.	D	26.	A	C	36.	N	D
7.	B		17.	I	27.	E	C	37.	D	L
8.	E		18.	D	28.	P	C	38.	D	J
9.	E		19.	J	29.	C	B	39.	D	I
10.	H		20.	B	30.	L	C	40.	D	O

TEST 2

DIRECTIONS: Each question or incomplete statement is followed by several suggested answers or completions. Select the one that BEST answers the question or completes the statement. *PRINT THE LETTER OF THE CORRECT ANSWER IN THE SPACE AT THE RIGHT.*

Questions 1-16.

DIRECTIONS: Read each statement carefully. If you believe that the account should be debited, place a D for DEBIT in the space at the right. If you think it should be credited, place a C for CREDIT in the space at the right.

1.   When sales are made for cash, the sales account is (debited or credited).   1._____

2.   When sales are made on account, the customer's account is (debited or credited).   2._____

3.   When merchandise is purchased for cash, the purchases account is (debited or credited).   3._____

4.   The creditor's account is (debited cr credited) when payment is made on account.   4._____

5.   The sales account is (debited or credited) for the total of the amount column in the Sales Journal.   5._____

6.   The cash account is (debited or credited) for the total of the cash column in the Cash Receipts Journal.   6._____

7.   The purchases account is (debited or credited) for the total amount of the purchases column in the Purchases Journal.   7._____

8.   The accounts receivable account is (debited or credited) for the total amount of the Sales Journal.   8._____

9.   Each account in the Sales Journal is posted to the (debit or credit) of the customer's account.   9._____

10.   The total of the accounts payable column in the Cash Payments Journal is posted to the (debit or credit) of the accounts payable account.   10._____

11.   The total of the cash column in the Cash Payments Journal is posted to the (debit or credit) of the cash account.   11._____

12.   Each account with an amount entered in the General column of the Cash Receipts Journal is (debited or credited).   12._____

13. When the proprietor invests additional cash in the business, the capital account is (debited or credited).

13.____

14. When merchandise is purchased on account, the purchases account is (debited or credited).

14.____

15. When sales salaries are unpaid at the close of the fiscal period, the salaries payable account is (debited or credited).

15.____

16. When equipment is purchased on account, the creditor's account is (debited or credited).

16.____

Questions 17-30.

DIRECTIONS: The following figures have been taken from Income Statements. Certain figures have been omitted and letters have been substituted. Determine the CORRECT amounts that should be recorded for each of the letters and write this amount in the space at the right. Each line across the page is a separate income statement.

Sales	Beginning Inventory	Purchases	Closing Inventory	Cost of Goods Sold	Gross Profit	Expenses	Net Profit	Net Loss
22,000	8,000	12,000	A	15,000	B	4,000	C	
D	E	60,000	30,000	40,000	10,000	F		2,000
3,500	1,000	2,500	500	G	500	H	100	
7,500	500	I	2,000	J	1,000	800	K	
30,000	L	25,000	5,000	28,000	M	2,500		N

17. A   17.____

18. B   18.____

19. C   19.____

20. D   20.____

21. E   21.____

22. F   22.____

23. G   23.____

24. H   24.____

25. I   25.____

26. J   26.____

27. K   27.____

28. L   28.____

29. M   29.____

30. N   30.____

KEY (CORRECT ANSWERS)

1.	C	16.	C
2.	D	17.	5,000
3.	D	18.	7,000
4.	D	19.	3,000
5.	C	20.	50,000
6.	D	21.	10,0000
7.	D	22.	12,000
8.	D	23.	3,000
9.	D	24.	400
10.	D	25.	8,000
11.	C	26.	6,500
12.	C	27.	200
13.	C	28.	8,000
14.	D	29.	2,000
15.	C	30.	500

———

TEST 3

Questions 1-25

DIRECTIONS: Each of Questions 1 through 25 consists of a statement. You are to indicate whether the statement is TRUE (T) or FALSE (F). *PRINT THE LETTER OF THE CORRECT ANSWER IN THE SPACE AT THE RIGHT.*

1. One of the primary objectives of the proprietor of a business is to increase his proprietorship by earning a profit.   1.____

2. The length of time covered by the Income and Expense Statement is of no importance or significance.   2.____

3. The length of time covered by the Balance Sheet is of no importance or significance.   3.____

4. When a customer takes advantage of a cash discount, the amount of cash received is more than the amount of the invoice for which payment is received.   4.____

5. Posting of column totals from the Cash Receipts Journal to the General Ledger is done each day.   5.____

6. After the adjustments have been entered in their appropriate column in the worksheet, their equality is proved by adding the columns.   6.____

7. The amount of unsold merchandise is found by subtracting the merchandise sales from the merchandise purchased.   7.____

8. In the Income and Expense Statement, the sales minus the cost of goods sold equals the gross profit.   8.____

9. If the operating expenses exceed the gross profit, a net loss results.   9.____

10. Only asset, liability, and capital accounts appear in the post-closing trial balance.   10.____

11. The earning of a net profit by a business results in an increase in the net worth of the business.   11.____

12. If the assets of a business are less than the liabilities, the business is solvent.   12.____

13. Small business can use accounting and data processing machines to a better advantage than large businesses.   13.____

14. The adjusting entries can be prepared from the adjustment columns of the worksheet.

14.____

15. The amount of the supplies used during the fiscal period is credited to the supplies account at the close of the fiscal period.

15.____

16. If the credit side of the income and expense summary account is larger than the debit side, the difference is a net loss to the business.

16.____

17. The discount on sales is considered to be a part of the regular operating expenses of the business.

17.____

18. In writing off a customer's uncollectible amount, the allowance for bad debts in the General Ledger is credited.

18.____

19. The amount credited to the allowance for bad debts account is an estimated amount.

19.____

20. The allowance for depreciation account usually has a credit balance.

20.____

21. The time received for a fixed asset at the time it is replaced is always equal to its book value.

21.____

22. Prepaid expenses are sometimes called deferred credits to income.

22.____

23. Expenses that are incurred but not paid are termed accrued expenses.

23.____

24. Prepaid expenses may be shown on the balance sheet as a current asset.

24.____

25. Equipment is listed on the balance sheet as a fixed asset.

25.____

Questions 26-30.

DIRECTIONS: Questions 26 through 30 are to be answered by writing the CORRECT amount in the space at the right.

26. The office supplies account has a balance of $150 at the close of the fiscal period. The actual inventory of supplies is $60. What is the amount of supplies used during the period?

26.____

27. A company receives $490 in cash from a customer for the prompt payment of an invoice. Two percent was the discount. What was the original amount of the invoice?

27.____

28. The balance of the store supplies before adjustment is $400. The total cost of the store supplies on hand at the end of the period is $150. What is the amount of the adjusting entry?

28.____

29. What is the amount necessary to pay a $300 invoice, terms 3/10, 2/20, n/30, twelve days after date?

29.____

30. If equipment costing $1,500, with an estimated life of ten years, was purchased, what is the annual rate of depreciation?

30.____

_____

KEY (CORRECT ANSWERS)

1.	T	11.	T	21.	F
2.	F	12.	F	22.	F
3.	T	13.	F	23.	T
4.	F	14.	T	24.	T
5.	F	15.	T	25.	T
6.	T	16.	F	26.	$90
7.	F	17.	F	27.	$500
8.	T	18.	F	28.	$250
9.	T	19.	T	29.	$294
10.	T	20.	T	30.	10%

_____

TEST 4

DIRECTIONS: Each question or incomplete statement is followed by several suggested answers or completions. Select the one that BEST answers the question or completes the statement. *PRINT THE LETTER OF THE CORRECT ANSWER IN THE SPACE AT THE RIGHT.*

Questions 1-12.

DIRECTIONS: Each of Questions 1 through 12 consists of a statement. You are to indicate whether the statement is TRUE (T) or FALSE (F). *PRINT THE LETTER OF THE CORRECT ANSWER IN THE SPACE AT THE RIGHT.*

1. The supplies used during a fiscal period are shown on the balance sheet as a current asset.   1.____

2. If the assets and liabilities increase equally, the proprietorship also increases.   2.____

3. The Income and Expense Statement shows the results of business operations over a period of time.   3.____

4. An exchange of one asset for another asset of different value causes a change in the proprietorship.   4.____

5. The recording of allowance for depreciation actually results in writing down the asset values.   5.____

6. If the closing merchandise inventory is understated, the profit for the period will be understated.   6.____

7. If accrued salaries during a period are not recorded, the profit for the period will be overstated.   7.____

8. If sales returns are understated during a fiscal period, the profit for that period will be understated.   8.____

9. Unpaid salaries should be added to the salaries for the period before the profit for the period is figured.   9.____

10. When posting the Sales Journal, each item is posted separately to the accounts receivable controlling account in the General Ledger.   10.____

11. A business is said to be solvent when it has a net profit for the period.   11.____

12. Accrued income is income earned but not received during a fiscal period.   12.____

Questions 13-30.

DIRECTIONS: Below is a list of terms with an accompanying list of definitions or explanations. In the space at the right, put the letter of the term in Column II which BEST explains the definition or explanation in Column I.

COLUMN I

COLUMN II

13. Entries needed to bring accounts up to date at the end of an accounting period

14. An entry in a book of original entry that has more than one debit or credit

15. An account used to summarize the income and expense data at the close of the fiscal period

16. An account with a balance that is partly a balance sheet amount and partly an income statement amount

17. Discount granted to a customer for early payment of his account

18. A journal designed for recording a particular type of transaction only

19. A ledger used for recording the details of a single account

20. An account in the general ledger that is supported by a subsidiary ledger

21. A list of individual account balances in a subsidiary ledger

22. Expense items bought and paid for, but not entirely consumed during the fiscal period

23. Expenses incurred but not paid during a fiscal period

24. The decrease in the value of a fixed asset due to wear and tear

25. The amount of unsold merchandise on hand

A. Abstract
B. Accrued expenses
C. Adjusting entries
D. Allowance for bad debts
E. Book value
F. Cash discount
G. Compound entry
H. Controlling account
I. Current asset
J. Depreciation
K. Fixed asset
L. General ledger
M. Income & expense summary
N. Merchandise inventory
O. Mixed account
P. Petty cash
Q. Prepaid expenses
R. Retail method
S. Special journal
T. Straight-line method
U. Subsidiary ledger
V. Voucher

13._____

14._____

15._____

16._____

17._____

18._____

19._____

20._____

21._____

22._____

23._____

24._____

25._____

26. Assets of a more or less permanent
    nature used in the business

26.____

27. The amount of estimated uncollecible
    accounts receivable.

27.____

28. The most commonly used method of
    computing depreciation

28.____

29. The difference between the original
    cost of an asset and its valuation amount

29.____

30. A written authorization required for each
    expenditure

30.____

KEY (CORRECT ANSWERS)

1.	F	11.	F	21.	A		
2.	F	12.	T	22.	Q		
3.	T	13.	C	23.	B		
4.	T	14.	G	24.	J		
5.	F	15.	M	25.	N		
6.	T	16.	O	26.	K		
7.	T	17.	F	27.	D		
8.	F	18.	S	28.	T		
9.	T	19.	U	29.	E		
10.	F	20.	H	30.	V		

TEST 5

Questions 1-12.

DIRECTIONS: Questions 1 through 12 are to be answered by writing the CORRECT amount in the space at the right.

1. If the purchases for the month were $500, the beginning inventory was $1,500, the ending inventory was $1,000, and the gross profit was $2,000, what were the sales?

1.____

2. If the gross profit for the period was $750 and the net profit was $250, what was the amount of the expenses?

2.____

3. Determine the amount of the cost of goods sold if the purchases for the month were $10,000, the beginning inventory was $3,000, and the ending inventory was $5,000.

3.____

4. A typewriter was purchased for $300 with an estimated life of five years. What is the book value at the end of the third year?

4.____

5. A delivery truck costs $3,000. Its book value at the end of the third year was $2,100. What is the amount of depreciation each year?

5.____

6. The assets on a Balance Sheet are $7,500. The liabilities are $4,500. What is the capital?

6.____

7. A check was received for $242.50 in payment of a sale amounting to $250 less discount. What is the percent of discount allowed?

7.____

8. The capital at the close of the fiscal period was $10,000. The liabilities were $12,000. What are the TOTAL assets?

8.____

9. A note is dated March 1 and is due in 60 days. What is its due date?

9.____

10. A note is dated January 30. It is due in one month. What is its due date?

10.____

11. What is the interest on a note for $500 with interest at 6% for sixty days?

11.____

12. What is the interest on a note for $800 with interest at 6% for 45 days?

12.____

Questions 13-15

DIRECTIONS: Each of Questions 13 through 25 consists of a statement. You are to indicate whether the statement is TRUE (T) or FALSE (F). *PRINT THE LETTER OF THE CORRECT ANSWER IN THE SPACE AT THE RIGHT.*

13. To determine the value of the merchandise available for sale, the purchases are added to the beginning merchandise inventory.

13.____

14. The closing merchandise inventory is shown on both the Balance Sheet and the Income and Expense Statement.   14.____

15. The allowance for bad debts account is closed into the income and expense summary account at the close of the fiscal period.   15.____

16. The accounts payable account shows the total amount owed to creditors and also shows how much is owed to each creditor.   16.____

17. Sales discount is usually subtracted from the sales in the Income and Expense Statement.   17.____

18. The use of controlling accounts increases the possibility of errors in preparing the trial balance.   18.____

19. The use of controlling accounts results in fewer accounts in the General Ledger.   19.____

20. The total of the schedule of accounts receivable should equal the balance of the accounts receivable account in the General Ledger.   20.____

21. Closing entries summarize in the income and expense summary account the income costs and expense for the fiscal period.   21.____

22. The post-closing trial balance is made before the Balance Sheet has been made.   22.____

23. The closing entries are recorded in the General Journal.   23.____

24. The debit balance of the equipment account should show the book value of the equipment on hand.   24.____

25. The balance of the allowance for depreciation of equipment account is shown on the Balance Sheet.   25.____

KEY (CORRECT ANSWERS)

1.	$3,000		11.	$5.00
2.	$500		12.	$6.00
3.	$8,000		13.	T
4.	$120		14.	T
5.	$300		15.	F
6.	$3,000		16.	F
7.	3%		17.	T
8.	$22,000		18.	F
9.	April 30		19.	T
10.	Feb. 28		20.	T

21.	T
22.	F
23.	T
24.	F
25.	T

EXAMINATION SECTION
TEST 1

DIRECTIONS: Each question or incomplete statement is followed by several suggested answers or completions. Select the one that BEST answers the question or completes the statement. *PRINT THE LETTER OF THE CORRECT ANSWER IN THE SPACE AT THE RIGHT.*

Questions 1-5.

DIRECTIONS: Questions 1 through 5 are to be answered on the basis of the statement account shown below.

STATEMENT OF ACCOUNT

Regal Tools, Inc.
136 Culver Street
Cranston, R.I. 02910

TO: Vista, Inc.   DATE: March 31
     572 No. Copeland Ave.
     Pawtucket, R.I. 02800

DATE	ITEM	CHARGES	PAYMENTS AND CREDITS	BALANCE
	Previous Balance			785.35
March 8	Payment		785.35	----
12	Invoice 17-582	550 --		550.00
17	Invoice 17-692	700 --		1250.00
31	Payment		550.00	700.00

PAY LAST AMOUNT SHOWN IN BALANCE COLUMN

1. Which company is the customer?   1._____

2. What total amount was charged by the customer during March?   2._____

3. How much does the customer owe on March 31?   3._____

4. On which accounting schedule would Vista list Regal?   4._____

5. The terms on invoice 17-582 were 3/20, n/45.   5._____
   What was the CORRECT amount for which the check should have been written when payment was made?

6. Which item is NOT a source document?   6.____
   A(n)

   A. invoice   B. magnetic tape
   C. punched card   D. telephone conversation

7. What is double-entry accounting?   7.____

   A. Journalizing and posting
   B. Recording debit and credit parts for a transaction
   C. Using carbon paper when preparing a source document
   D. Posting a debit or credit and computing the new account balance

8. The balance in the asset account Supplies is $600. An ending inventory shows $200 of   8.____
   supplies on hand.
   The adjusting entry should be

   A. debit Supplies Expense for $200, credit Supplies for $200
   B. credit Supplies Expense for $200, debit Supplies for $200
   C. debit Supplies Expense for $400, credit Supplies for $400
   D. credit Supplies Expense for $400, debit Supplies for $400

9. What is the purpose of preparing an Income Statement?   9.____
   To

   A. report the net income or net loss
   B. show the owner's claims against the assets
   C. prove that the accounting equation is in balance
   D. prove that the total debits equal the total credits

10. Which account does NOT belong on the Income Statement?   10.____

    A. Salaries Payable
    B. Rental Revenue
    C. Advertising Expense
    D. Sales Returns and Allowances

11. The source document for entries made in a Purchases Journal is a purchase   11.____

    A. order   B. requisition   C. invoice   D. register

12. A business check guaranteed for payment by the bank is called a   12.____

    A. bank draft   B. certified check
    C. cashier's check   D. personal check

13. The entry that closes the Purchases Account contains a   13.____

    A. debit to Purchases
    B. debit to Purchases Returns and Allowances
    C. credit to Purchases
    D. credit to Income and Expense Summary

14. Which account would NOT appear on a Balance Sheet?   14.____

    A. Office Equipment   B. Transportation In
    C. Mortgage Payable   D. Supplies on Hand

15. Which entry is made at the end of the fiscal period for the purpose of updating the Pre-   15.____
paid Insurance Account?
_____ entry.

    A. Correcting   B. Closing   C. Adjusting   D. Reversing

16. Which deduction from gross pay is NOT required by law?   16.____

    A. Hospitalization insurance
    B. FICA tax
    C. Federal income tax
    D. New York State income tax

17. What is the last date on which a 2 percent cash discount can be taken for an invoice   17.____
dated October 15 with terms of 2/10, n/30?

    A. October 15   B. October 17
    C. October 25   D. November 14

18. Which item on the bank reconciliation statement would require the business to record a   18.____
journal entry?
A(n)

    A. deposit in transit   B. outstanding check
    C. canceled check   D. bank service charge

19. Which is NOT an essential component of a computer?   19.____
A(n)

    A. input device   B. central processor
    C. output device   D. telecommunicator

20. Which group of accounts could appear on a post-closing trial balance?   20.____

    A. Petty Cash; Accounts Receivable; FICA Taxes Payable
    B. Office Furniture; Office Expense; Supplies on Hand
    C. Supplies Expense; Sales; Advertising Expense
    D. Sales Discount; Rent Expense; J. Smith, Drawing

21. The withdrawals of cash by the owner are recorded in the owner's drawing account as   21.____
a(n)

    A. adjusting entry   B. closing entry
    C. credit   D. debit

22. An account in the General Ledger which shows a total of a related Subsidiary Ledger is   22.____
referred to as a(n) _____ account.

    A. revenue   B. controlling
    C. temporary   D. owner's equity

23.

For Deposit Only
Anthony Bill

Which type of endorsement is shown above?

A. Restrictive
C. Full
B. Blank
D. Qualified

23.____

24. Which is a chronological record of all the transactions of a business?

A. Worksheet
C. Journal
B. Income Statement
D. Trial balance

24.____

25. Which error would NOT be revealed by the preparation of a trial balance?

A. Posting of an entire transaction more than once
B. Incorrectly pencil footing the balance of a general ledger account
C. Posting a debit of $320 as $230
D. Omitting an account with a balance

25.____

26. The Cash Receipts Journal is used to record the

A. purchase of merchandise for cash
B. purchase of merchandise on credit
C. sale of merchandise for cash
D. sale of merchandise on credit

26.____

27. On a systems flowchart, which symbol is commonly used to indicate the direction of the flow of work?
A(n)

A. arrow
B. circle
C. diamond
D. rectangle

27.____

28. Which account balance would be eliminated by a closing entry at the end of the fiscal period?

A. Office Equipment
C. Owner's Capital
B. Owner's Drawing
D. Mortgage Payable

28.____

29. In a data processing system, the handling and manipulation of data according to precise procedures is called

A. input
C. storage
B. processing
D. output

29.____

30. Which financial statement reflects the cumulative financial position of the business?

A. Bank statement
C. Trial balance
B. Income statement
D. Balance sheet

30.____

31. Which account should be credited when recording a cash proof showing an overage?   31.____

    A. Sales
    B. Cash
    C. Cash Short and Over
    D. Sales Returns and Allowances

32. In which section of the income statement would the purchases account be shown?   32.____

    A. Cost of Goods Sold   B. Income from Sales
    C. Operating Expenses   D. Other Expenses

33. What is an invoice?   33.____
    A(n)

    A. order for the shipment of goods
    B. order for the purchase of goods
    C. receipt for goods purchased
    D. statement listing goods purchased

34. A business uses a Sales Journal, a Purchases Journal, a Cash Receipts Journal, a Cash   34.____
Payments Journal, and a General Journal.
In which journal would a credit memorandum received from a creditor be recorded?
_____ Journal

    A. Sales   B. Purchases
    C. General   D. Cash Receipts

35. Which account is debited to record a weekly payroll?   35.____

    A. Employees Income Tax Payable
    B. FICA Taxes Payable
    C. General Expense
    D. Salaries Expense

KEY (CORRECT ANSWERS)

1. Vista, Inc.
2. $1,250
3. $700
4. Accts. Payable
5. $533.50

6. D
7. B
8. C
9. A
10. A

11. C
12. B
13. C
14. D
15. C

16. A
17. C
18. D
19. D
20. A

21. D
22. B
23. A
24. C
25. A

26. C
27. A
28. B
29. B
30. D

31. C
32. A
33. D
34. C
35. D

EXAMINATION SECTION
TEST 1

DIRECTIONS: Each question or incomplete statement is followed by several suggested answers or completions. Select the one that BEST answers the question or completes the statement. *PRINT THE LETTER OF THE CORRECT ANSWER IN THE SPACE AT THE RIGHT.*

1. In the preparation of a balance sheet, failure to consider the inventory of office supplies will result in _____ assets and _____.   1._____

   A. overstating; overstating liabilities
   B. understating; overstating capital
   C. understating; understating capital
   D. overstating; understating liabilities

2. The annual federal unemployment tax is paid by the   2._____

   A. employer *only*
   B. employee *only*
   C. employer and the employee equally
   D. employee, up to a maximum of 30 cents per week, and the balance is paid by the employer

3. Which are NORMALLY considered as current assets?   3._____

   A. Bank overdrafts   B. Prepaid expenses
   C. Accrued expenses   D. Payroll taxes

4. What type of ledger account is a summary of a number of accounts in another ledger? The _____ account.   4._____

   A. controlling   B. subsidiary
   C. asset   D. proprietorship

5. The PRIMARY purpose of a petty cash fund is to   5._____

   A. provide a fund for paying all miscellaneous expenses
   B. take the place of the cash account
   C. provide a common drawing fund for the owners of the business
   D. avoid entering a number of small amounts in the Cash Payments Journal

6. In the absence of a written agreement, profits in a partnership would be divided   6._____

   A. in proportion to the investment of the partners
   B. on an equitable basis depending on the time and effort spent by the partners
   C. equally
   D. on a ratio of investment basis, giving the senior partner preference

7. Which account represents a subtraction or decrease to an income account?   7._____

   A. Purchase Returns & Allowances
   B. Sales Returns & Allowances
   C. Freight In
   D. Prepaid Rent

8. If the Interest Expense account showed a debit balance of $210 as of December 31, and   8._____
$40 of this amount was prepaid on Notes Payable, which statement is CORRECT as of
December 31?

    A. Prepaid Interest of $170 should be shown as a deferred expense in the balance
       sheet.
    B. Interest Expense should be shown in the Income Statement as $210.
    C. Prepaid Interest of $40 should be listed as a deferred credit to income in the bal-
       ance sheet.
    D. Interest Expense should be shown in the Income Statement as $170.

9. When prices are rising, which inventory-valuation method results in the LOWEST inven-   9._____
tory value?

    A. FIFO   B. LIFO
    C. Average cost   D. Declining balance

10. Which of the following is a CORRECT procedure in preparing a bank reconciliation?   10._____

    A. Deposits in transit should be added to the cash balance on the books, and out-
       standing checks should be deducted from the cash balance on the bank state-
       ment.
    B. The cash balance on the bank statement and the cash balance on the books
       should be equal if there are deposits in transit and outstanding checks.
    C. Outstanding checks should be deducted from the cash balance on the books.
    D. Any service charge should be deducted from the check stub balance.

11. Which ratio indicates that there may NOT be enough on hand to meet current obliga-   11._____
tions?

    A. $\dfrac{\text{fixed assets}}{\text{fixed liabilities}} = \dfrac{2}{3}$ B. $\dfrac{\text{total assets}}{\text{total obligations}} = \dfrac{3}{5}$

    C. $\dfrac{\text{current assets}}{\text{current liabilities}} = \dfrac{1}{3}$ D. $\dfrac{\text{current assets}}{\text{fixed liabilities}} = \dfrac{1}{2}$

12. Which asset is NOT subject to depreciation?   12._____

    A. Factory equipment   B. Land
    C. Buildings   D. Machinery

13. Which form is prepared to verify that the total of the account balances in the Customers   13._____
Ledger agrees with the balance in the controlling account in the General Ledger?

    A. Worksheet
    B. Schedule of accounts payable
    C. Schedule of accounts receivable
    D. Trial balance

14. If the merchandise inventory on hand at the end of the year was overstated, what will be the result of this error?   14.____

    A. *Understatement* of income for the year
    B. *Overstatement* of income for the year
    C. *Understatement* of assets at the end of the year
    D. No effect on income or assets

15. Working capital is found by subtracting the total current liabilities from the total   15.____

    A. fixed liabilities   B. fixed assets
    C. current income   D. current assets

16. Which is the CORRECT procedure for calculating the rate of merchandise turnover?   16.____

    A. Gross Sales divided by Net Sales
    B. Cost of Sales divided by Average Inventory
    C. Net Purchases divided by Average Inventory
    D. Gross Purchases divided by Net Purchases

17. The books of the Atlas Cement Corporation show a net profit of $142,000.   17.____
To close the Profit and Loss account of the corporation at the end of the year, the account CREDITED should be

    A. Earned Surplus   B. Capital Stock
    C. C. Atlas, Capital   D. C. Atlas, Personal

18. The bank statement at the end of the month indicated a bank charge for printing a new checkbook.   18.____
How is this information recorded?
Debit

    A. Cash and credit Office Supplies
    B. Office Supplies and credit the Bank Charges
    C. the Bank Charges and credit Office Supplies
    D. Miscellaneous Expense and credit Cash

19. The Allowance for Doubtful Accounts appears on the balance sheet as a deduction from   19.____

    A. Accounts Receivable   B. Notes Receivable
    C. Accounts Payable   D. Notes Payable

20. The Tucker Equipment Corporation had a $45,000 profit for the year ended December 31.   20.____
Which would be the PROPER entry to close the Income and Expense account at the end of the year?
Debit Income and Expense Summary; credit

    A. Tucker, Capital   B. Tucker, Drawing
    C. Retained Earnings   D. Capital Stock

21. A failure to record a purchases invoice would be discovered when the   21.____

    A. monthly statement of account is sent to the customer
    B. check is received from the customer
    C. check is sent to the creditor
    D. statement of account is received from the creditor

22. Which General Ledger account would appear in a post-closing trial balance?   22.____

    A. Notes Receivable   B. Bad Debts Expense
    C. Sales Discount   D. Fee Income

23. Which deduction is affected by the number of exemptions claimed?   23.____

    A. State Disability   B. State income tax
    C. FICA tax   D. Workers' Compensation

24. The face value of a 60-day, 12% promissory note is $900.   24.____
The maturity value of this note will be

    A. $909   B. $900   C. $918   D. $1,008

25. An invoice dated March 10, terms 2/10, n/30, should be paid no later than   25.____

    A. March 20   B. March 31   C. April 9   D. April 10

KEY (CORRECT ANSWERS)

1. C			11. C	
2. A			12. B	
3. B			13. C	
4. A			14. B	
5. D			15. D	
6. C			16. B	
7. B			17. A	
8. D			18. D	
9. B			19. A	
10. D			20. C	

21. D
22. A
23. B
24. C
25. C

TEST 2

DIRECTIONS: Each question or incomplete statement is followed by several suggested answers or completions. Select the one that BEST answers the question or completes the statement. *PRINT THE LETTER OF THE CORRECT ANSWER IN THE SPACE AT THE RIGHT.*

1. Which is NOT an essential element of a computer system?   1.____

   A. Input   B. Central processing unit
   C. Verifier   D. Output

2. The general ledger account that would NOT appear in a post-closing trial balance would be   2.____

   A. Cash   B. Accounts Payable
   C. Furniture and Fixtures   D. Sales Income

3. Ralph Hanley, age 45, supports his wife and three children. Mr. Hanley is the only member of the family required to file an income tax return. What is the MAXIMUM number of exemptions he can claim?   3.____

   A. One   B. Five   C. Three   D. Four

4. The cost of a fixed asset minus the allowance for depreciation (accumulated depreciation) is the _____ value.   4.____

   A. market   B. cost   C. liquidation   D. book

5. The form used by a bookkeeper in summarizing adjustments and information which will be used in preparing statements is called a   5.____

   A. journal   B. balance sheet
   C. ledger   D. worksheet

6. When a large number of transactions of a particular kind are to be entered in bookkeeping records, it is USUALLY advisable to use   6.____

   A. cash records   B. controlling accounts
   C. special journals   D. special ledgers

7. The petty cash book shows a petty cash balance of $9.80 on May 31. The petty cash box contains only $9.10. What account will be debited to record the $.70 difference?   7.____

   A. Cash   B. Petty Cash
   C. Cash Short and Over   D. Petty Cash Expense

8. The ONLY difference between the books of a partnership and those of a sole proprietorship appears in the _____ accounts.   8.____

   A. proprietorship   B. liability
   C. asset   D. expense

9. The earnings of a corporation are FIRST recorded as a credit to an account called   9.____

   A. Dividends Payable   B. Capital Stock Authorized
   C. Retained Earnings   D. Profit and Loss Summary

10. A firm purchased a new delivery truck for $2,900 and sold it four years later for $500. The
    Allowance for Depreciation of Delivery Equipment account was credited for $580 at the
    end of each of the four years.
    When the machine was sold, there was a
    10.____

    A. loss of $80   B. loss of $1,820
    C. loss of $2,400   D. gain of $80

11. FICA taxes are paid by
    11.____

    A. employees *only*
    B. employers *only*
    C. both employees and employers
    D. neither employees nor employers

12. Which phase of the data processing cycle is the SAME as calculating net pay in a man-
    ual system?
    12.____

    A. Input   B. Processing   C. Storing   D. Output

13. Which error will cause the trial balance to be out of balance?
    13.____

    A. A sales invoice for $60 was entered in the Sales Journal for $600.
    B. A credit to office furniture in the journal was posted as a credit to office machines in
       the ledger.
    C. A debit to advertising expense in the journal was posted as a debit to miscella-
       neous expense in the ledger.
    D. A debit to office equipment in the journal was posted as a credit to office equipment
       in the ledger.

14. The collection of a bad debt previously written off will result in a(n)
    14.____

    A. *decrease* in assets   B. *decrease* in capital
    C. *increase* in assets   D. *increase* in liabilities

15. Which account does NOT belong in the group?
    15.____

    A. Notes Receivable   B. Building
    C. Office Equipment   D. Delivery Truck

16. The adjusting entry to record the estimated bad debts is debit _____ and credit
    _____.
    16.____

    A. Allowance for Bad Debts; Bad Debts Expense
    B. Bad Debts Expense; Allowance for Bad Debts
    C. Allowance for Bad Debts; Accounts Receivable
    D. Bad Debts Expense; Accounts Receivable

17. At the end of the year, which account should be closed into the income and expense
    summary?
    17.____

    A. Freight In   B. Allowance for Doubtful Accounts
    C. Notes Receivable   D. Petty Cash

18. Which form is prepared to aid in verifying that the customer's account balances in the customer's ledger agree with the balance in the Accounts Receivable account in the general ledger?

    A. Worksheet
    B. Schedule of Accounts Payable
    C. Schedule of Accounts Receivable
    D. Trial Balance

18.____

19. In the preparation of an income statement, failure to consider accrued wages will result in

    A. *overstating* operating expense and understating net profit
    B. *overstating* net profit *only*
    C. *understating* operating expense and overstating net profit
    D. *understating* operating expense *only*

19.____

20. The CORRECT formula for determining the rate of merchandise turnover is

    A. cost of goods sold divided by average inventory
    B. net sales divided by net purchases
    C. gross sales divided by ending inventory
    D. average inventory divided by cost of goods sold

20.____

21. A legal characteristic of a corporation is _____ liability.

    A. contingent   B. limited
    C. unlimited   D. deferred

21.____

22. A customer's check you had deposited is returned to you by the bank labeled *Dishonored*.
What entries would be made as a result of this action? Debit _____ and credit _____.

    A. cash; customer's account
    B. miscellaneous expense; cash
    C. customer's account; capital
    D. customer's account; cash

22.____

23. The TOTAL capital of a corporation may be found by adding

    A. assets and liabilities
    B. assets and capital stock
    C. liabilities and capital stock
    D. earned surplus and capital stock

23.____

24. The source of an entry made in the Petty Cash book is the

    A. general ledger   B. voucher
    C. register   D. general journal

24.____

25. Which account is debited to record interest earned but not yet due?

    A. Deferred Interest
    B. Interest Receivable
    C. Interest Income
    D. Income and Expense Summary

25.____

KEY (CORRECT ANSWERS)

1. C	11. C
2. D	12. B
3. B	13. D
4. D	14. C
5. D	15. A
6. C	16. B
7. C	17. A
8. A	18. C
9. C	19. C
10. A	20. A

21. B
22. D
23. D
24. B
25. B

———

TEST 3

DIRECTIONS: Each question or incomplete statement is followed by several suggested answers or completions. Select the one that BEST answers the question or completes the statement. *PRINT THE LETTER OF THE CORRECT ANSWER IN THE SPACE AT THE RIGHT.*

1. Which reason should NOT generally be used by an employer when making a hiring decision?
   An applicant('s)

   A. resume reveals a lack of job-related skills
   B. attendance record on a previous job is poor
   C. has improperly prepared the job application
   D. is married

   1._____

2. Graves, Owens, and Smith formed a partnership and invested $15,000 each. If the firm made a profit of $18,000 last year and profits and losses were shared equally, what was Owens' share of the net profit?

   A. $1,000   B. $5,000   C. $6,000   D. $9,000

   2._____

3. The bank statement balance of the Bedford Co. on May 31 was $3,263.28. The checkbook balance was $3,119.06. A reconciliation showed that the outstanding checks totaled $147.22 and that there was a bank service charge of $3.00. The CORRECT checkbook balance should be

   A. $3,260.28   B. $3,122.06   C. $3,116.06   D. $3,266.28

   3._____

4. Which account is shown in a post-closing trial balance?

   A. Prepaid Insurance   B. Fees Income
   C. Purchases   D. Freight In

   4._____

5. A check endorsed *For deposit only (signed) Samuel Jones* is an example of a _____ endorsement.

   A. full   B. blank   C. complete   D. restrictive

   5._____

6. The selling price of a share of stock as published in a daily newspaper is called the _____ value.

   A. book   B. face   C. par   D. market

   6._____

7. Which is obtained by dividing the cost of goods sold by the average inventory?

   A. Current ratio
   B. Merchandise inventory turnover
   C. Average rate of mark-up
   D. Acid-test ratio

   7._____

8. A Suzuki truck costing $39,000 is expected to have a useful life of six years and a salvage value of $3,000.
   If $6,000 is debited to the depreciation expense account each year for six years, what method of depreciation is used?

   A. Units of production   B. Straight line
   C. Declining balance   D. Sum of the years digits

   8._____

9. Which form is prepared to aid in verifying that the customer's account balances in the customer's ledger agree with the balance in the Accounts Receivable account in the General Ledger?

    A. Worksheet
    B. Schedule of Accounts Payable
    C. Schedule of Accounts Receivable
    D. Trial Balance

9.____

10. In the preparation of a balance sheet, failure to consider commissions owed to salespersons will result in _____ liabilities and _____ capital.

    A. understating; overstating
    B. understating; understating
    C. overstating; overstating
    D. overstating; understating

10.____

11. A financial statement generated by a computer is an example of a(n)

    A. audit trail   B. output
    C. input   D. program

11.____

12. Merchandise was sold for $150 cash plus a 3% sales tax.
The CORRECT credit(s) should be

    A. Sales Income $150, Sales Taxes Payable $4.50
    B. Sales Income $154.50
    C. Merchandise $150, Sales Taxes Payable $4.50
    D. Sales Income $150

12.____

13. The bookkeeper should prepare a bank reconciliation MAINLY to determine

    A. which checks are outstanding
    B. whether the checkbook balance and the bank statement balance are in agreement
    C. the total amount of checks written during the month
    D. the total amount of cash deposited during the month

13.____

14. Which is the CORRECT procedure for calculating the rate of merchandise turnover?

    A. Gross Sales divided by Net Sales
    B. Cost of Goods Sold divided by Average Inventory
    C. Net Purchases divided by Average Inventory
    D. Gross Purchases divided by Net Purchases

14.____

15. Which previous job should be listed FIRST on a job application form?
The

    A. least recent job   B. most recent job
    C. job you liked best   D. job which paid the most

15.____

16. Failure to record cash sales will result in

    A. *overstatement* of profit
    B. *understatement* of profit
    C. *understatement* of liabilities
    D. *overstatement* of capital

16.____

17. When a fixed asset is repaired, the cost of the repairs should be _____ account.   17.____

   A. *debited* to the asset
   B. *debited* to the expense
   C. *credited* to the proprietor's capital
   D. *credited* to the asset

18. The form used by a bookkeeper to summarize information which will be used in preparing financial statements is called a   18.____

   A. journal   B. balance sheet
   C. ledger   D. worksheet

19. Which type of ledger account is a summary of a number of accounts in another ledger? _____ account.   19.____

   A. Controlling   B. Subsidiary
   C. Asset   D. Proprietorship

20. What is the summary entry on the Purchases Journal?   20.____
   Debit _____ and credit _____.

   A. Accounts Payable; Merchandise Purchases
   B. Accounts Receivable; Merchandise Purchases
   C. Merchandise Purchases; Accounts Receivable
   D. Merchandise Purchases; Accounts Payable

21. The source document for entries made in the Sales Journal is a(n)   21.____

   A. credit memo   B. statement of accounts
   C. invoice   D. bill of lading

22. A Trial Balance which is in balance would NOT reveal the   22.____

   A. omission of the credit part of an entry
   B. posting of the same debit twice
   C. omission of an entire transaction
   D. omission of an account with a balance

23. A financial statement prepared by a computerized accounting system is an example of   23.____

   A. input   B. output
   C. flowcharting   D. programming

24. The form which the payroll clerk gives to each employee to show gross earnings and taxes withheld for the year is a   24.____

   A. W-2   B. W-3   C. W-4   D. 1040

25. Who would be the LEAST appropriate reference on an application for a job? A   25.____

   A. relative
   B. guidance counselor
   C. former employer
   D. prominent member of the community

KEY (CORRECT ANSWERS)

1.	D		11.	B
2.	C		12.	A
3.	C		13.	B
4.	A		14.	B
5.	D		15.	B
6.	D		16.	B
7.	B		17.	B
8.	B		18.	D
9.	C		19.	A
10.	A		20.	D

21.	C
22.	C
23.	B
24.	A
25.	A

EXAMINATION SECTION
TEST 1

DIRECTIONS: Each question or incomplete statement is followed by several suggested answers or completions. Select the one that BEST answers the question or completes the statement. *PRINT THE LETTER OF THE CORRECT ANSWER IN THE SPACE AT THE RIGHT.*

Questions 1-5

DIRECTIONS: Questions 1 through 5 are to be answered on the basis of the extracts from Federal income tax withholding and social security tax tables shown below. These tables indicate the amounts which must be withheld from the employee's salary by his employer for Federal income tax and for social security. They are based on weekly earnings.

INCOME TAX WITHHOLDING TABLE							
The wages are		And the number of withholding allowances is					
		5	6	7	8	9	10 or
At	But less						more
least	than	The amount of Income tax to be withheld shall be					
$300	$320	$24.60	$19.00	$13.80	$ 8.60	$ 4.00	$ 0
320	340	28.80	22.80	17.40	12.20	7.00	2.80
340	360	33.00	27.00	21.00	15.80	10.60	5.60
360	380	37.20	31.20	25.20	19.40	14.20	9.00
380	400	41.40	35.40	29.40	23.40	17.80	12.60
400	420	45.60	39.60	33.60	27.60	21.40	16.20
420	440	49.80	43.80	37.80	31.80	25.60	19.80
440	460	54.00	48.00	42.00	36.00	29.80	23.80
460	480	58.20	52.20	46.20	40.20	34.00	38.00
480	500	62.40	56.40	50.40	44.40	38.20	32.20

SOCIAL SECURITY TABLE					
WAGES			WAGES		Tax
At least	But less than	Tax to be withheld	At least	But less than	to be withheld
$333.18	$333.52	$19.50	$336.60	$336.94	$19.70
333.52	333.86	19.52	336.94	337.28	19.72
333.86	334.20	19.54	337.28	337.62	19.74
334.20	334.54	19.56	337.62	337.96	19.76
334.54	334.88	19.58	337.96	338.30	19.78
334.88	335.22	19.60	338.30	338.64	19.80
335.22	335.56	19.62	338.64	338.98	19.82
335.56	335.90	19.64	338.98	339.32	19.84
335.90	336.24	19.66	339.32	339.66	19.86
336.24	336.60	19.68	339.66	340.00	19.88

1. If an employee has a weekly wage of $379.50 and claims 6 withholding allowances, the amount of income tax to be withheld is

   A. $27.00   B. $31.20   C. $35.40   D. $37.20

   1.____

2. An employee had wages of $335.60 for one week.
   With eight withholding allowances claimed, how much income tax will be withheld from his salary?

   A. $8.60   B. $12.20   C. $13.80   D. $17.40

   2.____

3. How much social security tax will an employee with weekly wages of $335.60 pay?

   A. $19.60   B. $19.62   C. $19.64   D. $19.66

   3.____

4. Mr. Wise earns $339.80 a week and claims seven withholding allowances.
   What is his take-home pay after income tax and social security tax are deducted?

   A. $300.32   B. $302.52   C. $319.92   D. $322.40

   4.____

5. If an employee pays $19.74 in social security tax and claims eight withholding allowances, the amount of income tax that should be withheld from his wages is

   A. $8.60   B. $12.20   C. $13.80   D. $15.80

   5.____

6. A fundamental rule of bookkeeping states that an individual's assets equal his liabilities plus his proprietorship (ASSETS = LIABILITIES + PROPRIETORSHIP).
   Which of the following statements logically follows from this rule?

   A. ASSETS = PROPRIETORSHIP - LIABILITIES
   B. LIABILITIES = ASSETS + PROPRIETORSHIP
   C. PROPRIETORSHIP = ASSETS - LIABILITIES
   D. PROPRIETORSHIP = LIABILITIES + ASSETS

   6.____

7. Mr. Martin's assets consist of the following:
        Cash on hand: $5,233.74
        Furniture: $4,925.00
        Government Bonds: $5,500.00
   What are his TOTAL assets?

   A. $10,158.74   B. $10,425.00
   C. $10,733.74   D. $15,658.74

   7.____

8. If Mr. Mitchell has $627.04 in his checking account and then writes three checks for $241.75, $13.24, and $102.97, what will be his new balance?

   A. $257.88   B. $269.08   C. $357.96   D. $369.96

   8.____

9. An employee's net pay is equal to his total earnings less all deductions.
   If an employee's total earnings in a pay period are $497.05, what is his NET pay if he has the following deductions:
   Federal income tax, $90.32; FICA, $28.74; State tax, $18.79; City tax, $7.25; Pension, $1.88?

   A. $351.17   B. $351.07   C. $350.17   D. $350.07

   9.____

10. A petty cash fund had an opening balance of $85.75 on December 1. Expenditures of $23.00, $15.65, $5.23, $14.75, and $26.38 were made out of this fund during the first 14 days of the month. Then, on December 17, another $38.50 was added to the fund. If additional expenditures of $17.18, $3.29, and $11.64 were made during the remainder of the month, what was the FINAL balance of the petty cash fund at the end of December?   10._____

   A. $6.93   B. $7.13   C. $46.51   D. $91.40

Questions 11-15.

DIRECTIONS: Questions 11 through 15 are to be answered on the basis of the following instructions.

The chart below is used by the loan division of a city retirement system for the following purposes: (1) to calculate the monthly payment a member must pay on an outstanding loan; (2) to calculate how much a member owes on an outstanding loan after he has made a number of payments.

To calculate the amount a member must pay each month in repaying his loan, look at Column II on the chart. You will notice that each entry in Column II corresponds to a number appearing under the *Months* column; for example, 1.004868 corresponds to 1 month, 0.503654 corresponds to 2 months, etc. To calculate the amount a member must pay each month, use the following procedure: multiply the amount of the loan by the entry in Column II which corresponds to the number of months over which the loan will be paid back. For example, if a loan of $200 is taken out for six months, multiply $200 by 0.169518, the entry in Column II which corresponds to six months.

In order to calculate the balance still owed on an outstanding loan, multiply the monthly payment by the number in Column I which corresponds to the number of monthly payments which remain to be paid on the loan. For example, if a member is supposed to pay $106.00 a month for twelve months, after seven payments, five monthly payments remain. To calculate the balance owed on the loan at this point, multiply the $106.00 monthly payment by 4.927807, the number in Column I that corresponds to five months.

Months	Column I	Column II
1	0.995156	1.004868
2	1.985491	0.503654
3	2.971029	0.336584
4	3.951793	0.253050
5	4.927807	0.202930
6	5.899092	0.169518
7	6.865673	0.145652
8	7.827572	0.127754
9	8.784811	0.113833
10	9.737414	0.102697
11	10.685402	0.093586
12	11.628798	0.085993
13	12.567624	0.079570
14	13.501902	0.074064
15	14.431655	0.069292

11. If Mr. Carson borrows $1,500 for eight months, how much will he have to pay back each month?   11._____

    A. $187.16   B. $191.63   C. $208.72   D. $218.65

12. If a member borrows $2,400 for one year, the amount he will have to pay back each month is   12._____

    A. $118.78   B. $196.18   C. $202.28   D. $206.38

13. Mr. Elliott borrowed $1,700 for a period of fifteen months.
Each month he will have to pay back   13._____

    A. $117.80   B. $116.96   C. $107.79   D. $101.79

14. Mr. Aylward is paying back a thirteen-month loan at the rate of $173.13 a month.
If he has already made six monthly payments, how much does he owe on the outstanding loan?   14._____

    A. $1,027.39   B. $1,178.75   C. $1,188.65   D. $1,898.85

15. A loan was taken out for 15 months, and the monthly payment was $104.75.
After two monthly payments, how much was still owed on this loan?   15._____

    A. $515.79   B. $863.89   C. $1,116.76   D. $1,316.46

16. The ABC Corporation had a gross income of $125,500.00 in 2005. Of this, it paid 60% for overhead.
If the gross income for 2006 increased by $6,500 and the cost of overhead increased to 61% of gross income, how much more did it pay for overhead in 2006 than in 2005?   16._____

    A. $1,320   B. $5,220   C. $7,530   D. $8,052

17. After one year, Mr. Richards paid back a total of $1,695.00 as payment for a $1,500.00 loan. All the money paid over $1,500.00 was simple interest.
The interest charge was MOST NEARLY   17._____

    A. 13%   B. 11%   C. 9%   D. 7%

18. A checking account has a balance of $253.36.
If deposits of $36.95, $210.23, and $7.34 and withdrawals of $117.35, $23.37, and $15.98 are made, what is the NEW balance of the account?   18._____

    A. $155.54   B. $351.18   C. $364.58   D. $664.58

19. In 2005, the W Realty Company spent 27% of its income on rent.
If it earned $97,254.00 in 2005, the amount it paid for rent was   19._____

    A. $26,258.58   B. $26,348.58
    C. $27,248.58   D. $27,358.58

20. Six percent simple annual interest on $2,436.18 is MOST NEARLY   20._____

    A. $145.08   B. $145.17   C. $146.08   D. $146.17

21. Assume that the XYZ Company has $10,402.72 cash on hand. If it pays $699.83 of this for rent, the amount of cash on hand would be

    A. $9,792.89   B. $9,702.89
    C. $9,692.89   D. $9,602.89

21._____

22. On January 31, Mr. Warren's checking account had a balance of $933.68.
If he deposited $36.40 on February 2, $126.00 on February 9, and $90.02 on February 16, and wrote no checks during this period, what was the balance of his account on February 17?

    A. $680.26   B. $681.25   C. $1,186.10   D. $1,187.00

22._____

23. Multiplying a number by .75 is the same as

    A. *multiplying* it by 2/3   B. *dividing* it by 2/3
    C. *multiplying* it by 3/4   D. *dividing* it by 3/4

23._____

24. In City Agency A, 2/3 of the employees are enrolled in a retirement system. City Agency B has the same number of employees as Agency A, and 60% of these are enrolled in a retirement system.
If Agency A has a total of 660 employees, how many MORE employees does it have enrolled in a retirement system than does Agency B?

    A. 36   B. 44   C. 56   D. 66

24._____

25. Net Worth is equal to Assets minus Liabilities.
If, at the end of year, a textile company had assets of $98,695.83 and liabilities of $59,238.29, what was its net worth?

    A. $38,478.54   B. $38,488.64
    C. $39,457.54   D. $48,557.54

25._____

KEY (CORRECT ANSWERS)

1.	B	11.	B
2.	B	12.	D
3.	C	13.	A
4.	B	14.	C
5.	B	15.	D
6.	C	16.	B
7.	D	17.	A
8.	B	18.	B
9.	D	19.	A
10.	B	20.	D

21.	B
22.	C
23.	C
24.	B
25.	C

TEST 2

DIRECTIONS: Each question or incomplete statement is followed by several suggested answers or completions. Select the one that BEST answers the question or completes the statement. *PRINT THE LETTER OF THE CORRECT ANSWER IN THE SPACE AT THE RIGHT.*

Questions 1-10.

DIRECTIONS: Questions 1 through 10 below present the identification numbers, initials, and last names of employees enrolled in a city retirement system. You are to choose the option (A, B, C, or D) that has the IDENTICAL identification number, initials, and last name as those given in each question.

Sample Question
B145698 JL Jones
  A. B146798 JL Jones
  C. P145698 JL Jones
               B. B145698 JL Jonas
               D. B145698 JL Jones

The correct answer is D. Only Option D shows the identification number, initials, and last name exactly as they are in the sample question. Options A, B, and C have errors in the identification number or last name.

1. J297483 PL Robinson

    A. J294783 PL Robinson   B. J297483 PL Robinson
    C. J297483 PI Robinson   D. J297843 PL Robinson   1._____

2. S497662 JG Schwartz

    A. S497662 JG Schwarz   B. S497762 JG Schwartz
    C. S497662 JG Schwartz   D. S497663 JG Schwartz   2._____

3. G696436 LN Alberton

    A. G696436 LM Alberton   B. G696436 LN Albertson
    C. G696346 LN Albertson   D. G696436 LN Alberton   3._____

4. R774923 AD Aldrich

    A. R774923 AD Aldrich   B. R744923 AD Aldrich
    C. R774932 AP Aldrich   D. R774932 AD Allrich   4._____

5. N239638 RP Hrynyk

    A. N236938 PR Hrynyk   B. N236938 RP Hrynyk
    C. N239638 PR Hrynyk   D. N239638 RP Hrynyk   5._____

6. R156949 LT Carlson

    A. R156949 LT Carlton   B. R156494 LT Carlson
    C. R159649 LT Carlton   D. R156949 LT Carlson   6._____

7. T524697 MN Orenstein

    A. T524697 MN Orenstein   B. T524967 MN Orinstein
    C. T524697 NM Ornstein   D. T524967 NM Orenstein   7._____

8.   L346239 JD Remsen   8.____

    A.   L346239 JD Remson   B.   L364239 JD Remsen
    C.   L346329 JD Remsen   D.   L346239 JD Remsen

9.   P966438 SB Rieperson   9.____

    A.   P996438 SB Reiperson   B.   P966438 SB Reiperson
    C.   R996438 SB Rieperson   D.   P966438 SB Rieperson

10.   D749382 CD Thompson   10.____

    A.   P749382 CD Thompson   B.   D749832 CD Thomsonn
    C.   D749382 CD Thompson   D.   D749823 CD Thomspon

Questions 11-20.

DIRECTIONS: Assume that each of the capital letters in the table below represents the name of an employee enrolled in the city's employees' personnel system. The number directly beneath the letter represents the agency for which the employee works, and the small letter directly beneath represents the code for the employee's account.

Name of Employee	L	O	T	Q	A	M	R	N	C
Agency	3	4	5	9	8	7	2	1	6
Account Code	r	f	b	i	d	t	g	e	n

In each of the following Questions 11 through 20, the agency code numbers and the account code letters in Columns 2 and 3 should correspond to the capital letters in Column 1 and should be in the same consecutive order. For each question, look at each column carefully and mark your answer as follows:

If there are one or more errors in Column 2 *only,* mark your answer A.
If there are one or more errors in Column 3 *only,* mark your answer B.
If there are one or more errors in Column 2 and one or more errors in Column 3, mark your answer C.
If there are NO errors n either column, mark your answer D.

SAMPLE QUESTION

Column 1	Column 2	Column 3
T Q L M O C	5 8 3 7 4 6	b i r t f n

In Column 2, the second agency code number (corresponding to letter Q) should be 9, not 8. Column 3 is coded correctly to Column 1. Since there is an error only in Column 2, the correct answer is A.

	COLUMN 1	COLUMN 2	COLUMN 3	
11.	QLNRCA	931268	iregnd	11.____
12.	NRMOTC	127546	egftbn	12.____
13.	RCTALM	265837	gndbrt	13.____
14.	TAMLON	578341	bdtrfe	14.____
15.	ANTORM	815427	debigt	15.____
16.	MRALON	728341	tgdrfe	16.____
17.	CTNQRO	657924	ndeigf	17.____
18.	QMROTA	972458	itgfbd	18.____
19.	RQMCOL	297463	gitnfr	19.____
20.	NOMRTQ	147259	eftgbi	20.____

Questions 21-25.

DIRECTIONS: Questions 21 through 25 are to be answered SOLELY on the basis of the following passage.

The city may issue its own bonds or it may purchase bonds as an investment. Bonds may be issued in various denominations, and the face value of the bond is its par value. Before purchasing a bond, the investor desires to know the rate of income that the investment will yield. In computing the yield on a bond, it is assumed that the investor will keep the bond until the date of maturity, except for callable bonds which are not considered in this passage. To compute exact yield is a complicated mathematical problem, and scientifically prepared tables are generally used to avoid such computation. However, the approximate yield can be computed much more easily. In computing approximate yield, the accrued interest on the date of purchase should be ignored because the buyer who pays accrued interest to the seller receives it again at the next interest date. Bonds bought at a premium (which cost more) yield a lower rate of income than the same bonds bought at par (face value), and bonds bought at a discount (which cost less) yield a higher rate of income than the same bonds bought at par.

21. An investor bought a $10,000 city bond paying 6% interest. Which of the following purchase prices would indicate that the bond was bought at a premium?

    A. $9,000   B. $9,400   C. $10,000   D. $10,600

21.____

22. During 2006, a particular $10,000 bond paying 7 1/2% sold at fluctuating prices. Which of the following prices would indicate that the bond was bought at a discount?

    A. $9,800   B. $10,000   C. $10,200   D. $10,750

22.____

23. A certain group of bonds was sold in denominations of $5,000, $10,000, $20,000, and   23.____
$50,000.
In the following list of four purchase prices, which one is MOST likely to represent a
bond sold at par value?

   A. $10,500   B $20,000   C. $22,000   D. $49,000

24. When computing the approximate yield on a bond, it is DESIRABLE to   24.____

   A. assume the bond was purchased at par
   B. consult scientifically prepared tables
   C. ignore accrued interest on the date of purchase
   D. wait until the bond reaches maturity

25. Which of the following is MOST likely to be an exception to the information provided in   25.____
the above passage?
Bonds

   A. purchased at a premium   B. sold at par
   C. sold before maturity   D. which are callable

_____

KEY (CORRECT ANSWERS)

1.	B		11.	D
2.	C		12.	C
3.	D		13.	B
4.	A		14.	A
5.	D		15.	B
6.	D		16.	D
7.	A		17.	C
8.	D		18.	D
9.	D		19.	A
10.	C		20.	D

21.	D
22.	A
23.	B
24.	C
25.	D

_____

TEST 3

DIRECTIONS: Each question or incomplete statement is followed by several suggested answers or completions. Select the one that BEST answers the question or completes the statement. *PRINT THE LETTER OF THE CORRECT ANSWER IN THE SPACE AT THE RIGHT.*

Questions 1-6.

DIRECTIONS: Questions 1 through 6 consist of computations of addition, subtraction, multiplication, and division. For each question, do the computation indicated, and choose the correct answer from the four choices given.

1. ADD: 8936
       7821
       8953
       4297
       9785
       6579

    A. 45371   B. 45381   C. 46371   D. 46381

1.____

2. SUBTRACT: 95,432
              67,596

    A. 27,836   B. 27,846   C. 27,936   D. 27,946

2.____

3. MULTIPLY: 987
             867

    A. 854609   B. 854729   C. 855709   D. 855729

3.____

4. DIVIDE: $59\overline{)321439.0}$

    A. 5438.1   B. 5447.1   C. 5448.1   D. 5457.1

4.____

5. DIVIDE: $.057\overline{)721}$

    A. 12,648.0   B. 12,648.1   C. 12,649.0   D. 12,649.1

5.____

6. ADD: 1/2 + 5/7

    A. 1 3/14   B. 1 2/7   C. 1 5/14   D. 1 3/7

6.____

7. If the total number of employees in one city agency increased from 1,927 to 2,006 during a certain year, the percentage increase in the number of employees for that year is MOST NEARLY

    A. 4%   B. 5%   C. 6%   D. 7%

7.____

8. During a single fiscal year, which totaled 248 workdays, one account clerk verified 1,488   8.____
   purchase vouchers. Assuming a normal work week of five days, what is the average
   number of vouchers verified by the account clerk in a one-week period during this fiscal
   year?

    A.   25   B.   30   C.   35   D.   40

9. If the city department of purchase bought 190 computers for $793.50 each and 208 com-   9.____
   puters for $839.90 each, the TOTAL price paid for these computers is

    A. $315,813.00   B. $325,464.20
    C. $334,278.20   D. $335.863.00

Questions 10-14.

DIRECTIONS: Questions 10 through 14 are to be answered SOLELY on the basis of the infor-
                mation given in the following paragraph.

     Since discounts are in common use in the commercial world and apply to purchases made
by government agencies as well as business firms, it is essential that individuals in both public
and private employment who prepare bills, check invoices, prepare payment vouchers, or write
checks to pay bills have an understanding of the terms used. These include cash or time discount, trade discount, and discount series. A cash or time discount offers a reduction in price to
the buyer for the prompt payment of the bill and is usually expressed as a percentage with a
time requirement, stated in days, within which the bill must be paid in order to earn the discount.
An example would be 3/10, meaning a 3% discount may be applied to the bill if the payment is
forwarded to the vendor within ten days. On an invoice, the cash discount terms are usually followed by the net terms, which is the time in days allowed for ordinary payment of the bill. Thus
3/10, Net 30 means that full payment is expected in thirty days if the cash discount of 3% is not
taken for having paid the bill within ten days. When the expression Terms Net Cash is listed or
a bill, it means that no deduction for early payment is allowed. A trade discount is normally
applied to list prices by a manufacturer to show the actual price to retailers so that they may
know their cost and determine markups that will allow them to operate competitively and at a
profit. A trade discount is applied by the seller to the list price and is independent of a cash or
time discount. Discounts may also be used by manufacturers to adjust prices charged to retailers without changing list prices. This is usually done by series discounting and is expressed as
a series of percentages. To compute a series discount, such as 40%, 20%, 10%, first apply the
40% discount to the list price, then apply the 20% discount to the remainder, and finally apply
the 10% discount to the second remainder.

10. According to the above passage, trade discounts are   10.____

    A.   applied by the buyer
    B.   independent of cash discounts
    C.   restricted to cash sales
    D.   used to secure rapid payment of bills

11. According to the above passage, if the sales terms 5/10, Net 60 appear on a bill in the   11.____
     amount of $100 dated December 5, 2006 and the buyer submits his payment on Decem-
     ber 15, 2006, his PROPER payment should be

    A. $60   B. $90   C. $95   D. $100

12. According to the above passage, if a manufacturer gives a trade discount of 40% for an item with a list price of $250 and the terms are Net Cash, the price a retail merchant is required to pay for this item is   12.____

   A. $250   B. $210   C. $150   D. $100

13. According to the above passage, a series discount of 25%, 20%, 10% applied to a list price of $200 results in an ACTUAL price to the buyer of   13.____

   A. $88   B. $90   C. $108   D. $110

14. According to the above passage, if a manufacturer gives a trade discount of 50% and the terms are 6/10, Net 30, the cost to a retail merchant of an item with a list price of $500 and for which he takes the time discount is   14.____

   A. $220   B. $235   C. $240   D. $250

Questions 15-22.

DIRECTIONS: Questions 15 through 22 each show in Column I the information written on five cards (lettered j, k, l, m, n) which have to be filed. You are to choose the option (lettered A, B, C, or D) in Column II which BEST represents the proper order of filing according to the information, rules, and sample question given below.

A file card record is kept of the work assignments for all the employees in a certain bureau. On each card is the employee's name, the date of work assignment, and the work assignment code number. The cards are to be filed according to the following rules:

FIRST: File in alphabetical order according to employee's name.

SECOND: When two or more cards have the same employee's name, file according to the assignment date, beginning with the earliest date.

THIRD: When two or more cards have the same employee's name and the same date, file according to the work assignment number beginning with the lowest number.

Column II shows the cards arranged in four different orders. Pick the option (A, B, C, or D) in Column II which shows the correct arrangement of the cards according to the above filing rules.

SAMPLE QUESTION

Column I
j. Cluney 4/8/02 (486503)
k. Roster 5/10/01 (246611)
l. Altool 10/15/02 (711433)
m. Cluney 12/18/02 (527610)
n. Cluney 4/8/02 (486500)

Column II
A. k, l, m, j, n
B. k, n, j, l, m
C. l, k, j, m, n
D. l, n, j, m, k

The correct way to file the cards is:

l. Altool 10/15/02 (711433)
n. Cluney 4/8/02 (486500)
j. Cluney 4/8/02 (486503)
m. Cluney 12/18/02 (527610)
k. Roster 5/10/01 (246611)

The correct filing order is shown by the letters l, n, j, m, k. The answer to the sample question is the letter D, which appears in front of the letters l, n, j, m, k in Column II.

COLUMN I	COLUMN II	
15. j. Smith 3/19/03 (662118) k. Turner 4/16/99 (481349) l. Terman 3/20/02 (210229) m. Smyth 3/20/02 (481359) n. Terry 5/11/01 (672123)	A. j, m, l, n, k B. j, l, n, m, k C. k, n, m, l, j D. j, n, k, l, m	15.____
16. j. Ross 5/29/02 (396118) k. Rosner 5/29/02 (439281) l. Rose 7/19/02 (723456) m. Rosen 5/29/03 (829692) n. Ross 5/29/02 (399118)	A. l, m, k, n, j B. m, l, k, n, j C. l, m, k, j, n D. m, l, j, n, k	16.____
17. j. Sherd 10/12/99 (552368) k. Snyder 11/12/99 (539286) l. Shindler 10/13/98 (426798) m. Scherld 10/12/99 (552386) n. Schneider 11/12/99 (798213)	A. n, m, k, j, l B. j, m, l, k, n C. m, k, n, j, l D. m, n, j, l, k	17.____
18. j. Carter 1/16/02 (489636) k. Carson 2/16/01 (392671) l. Carter 1/16/01 (486936) m. Carton 3/15/00 (489539) n. Carson 2/16/01 (392617)	A. k, n, j, l, m B. n, k, m, l, j C. n, k, l, j, m D. k, n, l, j, m	18.____
19. j. Thomas 3/18/99 (763182) k. Tompkins 3/19/00 (928439) l. Thomson 3/21/00 (763812) m. Thompson 3/18/99 (924893) n. Tompson 3/19/99 (928733)	A. m, l, j, k, n B. j, m, l, k, n C. j, l, n, m, k D. l, m, j, n, k	19.____
20. j. Breit 8/10/03 (345612) k. Briet 5/21/00 (837543) l. Bright 9/18/99 (931827) m. Breit 3/7/98 (553984) n. Brent 6/14/04 (682731)	A. m, j, n, k, l B. n, m, j, k, l C. m, j, k, l, n D. j, m, k, l, n	20.____
21. j. Roberts 10/19/02 (581932) k. Rogers 8/9/00 (638763) l. Rogerts 7/15/97 (105669) m. Robin 3/8/92 (287915) n. Rogers 4/2/04 (736921)	A. n, k, l, m, j B. n, k, l, j, m C. k, n, l, m, j D. j, m, k, n, l	21.____

	COLUMN I	COLUMN II	

22.   j. Hebert 4/28/02 (719468)   A. n, k, j, m, l   22.____

        k. Herbert 5/8/01 (938432)   B. j, l, n, k, m

        l. Helbert 9/23/04 (832912)   C. l, j, k, n, m

        m. Herbst 7/10/03 (648599)   D. l, j, n, k, m

        n. Herbert 5/8/01 (487627)

23. In order to pay its employees, the Convex Company obtained bills and coins in the following denominations: 23.____

Denomination	$20	$10	$5	$1	$.50	$.25	$.10	$.05	$.01
Number	317	122	38	73	69	47	39	25	36

What was the TOTAL amount of cash obtained?

A. $7,874.76   B. $7,878.00
C. $7,889.25   D. $7,924.35

24. H. Partridge receives a weekly gross salary (before deductions) of $596.25. Through   24.____
weekly payroll deductions of $19.77, he is paying back a loan he took from his pension fund.
If other fixed weekly deductions amount to $184.14, how much pay would Mr. Partridge take home over a period of 33 weeks?

A. $11,446.92   B. $12,375.69
C. $12,947.22   D. $19,676.25

25. Mr. Robertson is a city employee enrolled in a city retirement system. He has taken out a   25.____
loan from the retirement fund and is paying it back at the rate of $14.90 every two weeks.
In eighteen weeks, how much money will he have paid back on the loan?

A. $268.20   B. $152.80   C. $134.10   D. $67.05

26. In 2005, the Iridor Book Company had the following expenses: rent, $6,500; overhead,   26.____
$52,585; inventory, $35,700; and miscellaneous, $1,275.
If all of these expenses went up 18% in 2006, what would they TOTAL in 2006?

A. $17,290.80   B. $78,769.20
C. $96,060.00   D. $113,350.80

27. Ms. Ranier had a gross salary of $355.36, paid once every week.   27.____
If the deductions from each paycheck are $62.72, $25.13, $6.29, and $1.27, how much money would Ms. Ranier take home in four weeks?

A. $1,039.80   B. $1,421.44
C. $2,079.60   D. $2,842.88

28. Mr. Martin had a net income of $19,100 for the year. If he spent 34% on rent and house-   28.____
hold expenses, 3% on house furnishings, 25% on clothes, and 36% on food, how much was left for savings and other expenses?

A. $196.00   B. $382.00   C. $649.40   D. $1960.00

29. Mr. Elsberg can pay back a loan of $1,800 from the city employees' retirement system if   29.____
he pays back $36.69 every two weeks for two full years.
At the end of the two years, how much more than the original $1,800 he borrowed will
Mr. Elsberg have paid back?

   A. $53.94   B. $107.88   C. $190.79   D. $214.76

30. Mrs. Nusbaum is a city employee, receiving a gross salary (salary before deductions) of   30.____
$31,200. Every two weeks, the following deductions are taken out of her salary: Federal
Income Tax, $243.96; FICA, $66.39; State Tax, $44.58; City Tax, $20.91; Health
Insurance, $4.71.
If Mrs.Nusbaum's salary and deductions remained the same for a full calendar year,
what would her NET salary (gross salary less deductions) be in that year?

   A. $9,894.30   B. $21,305.70
   C. $28,118.25   D. $30,819.45

KEY (CORRECT ANSWERS)

1.	C	16.	C
2.	A	17.	D
3.	D	18.	C
4.	C	19.	B
5.	D	20.	A
6.	A	21.	D
7.	A	22.	B
8.	B	23.	A
9.	B	24.	C
10.	B	25.	C
11.	C	26.	D
12.	C	27.	A
13.	C	28.	B
14.	B	29.	B
15.	A	30.	B

READING COMPREHENSION
UNDERSTANDING AND INTERPRETING WRITTEN MATERIAL
EXAMINATION SECTION
TEST 1

DIRECTIONS: Each question or incomplete statement is followed by several suggested answers or completions. Select the one that BEST answers the question or completes the statement. *PRINT THE LETTER OF THE CORRECT ANSWER IN THE SPACE AT THE RIGHT.*

Questions 1-4.

DIRECTIONS: Questions 1 through 4 are to be answered SOLELY on the basis of the following paragraph.

An annual leave allowance, which combines leaves previously given for vacation, personal business, family illness, and other reasons shall be granted members. Calculation of credits for such leave shall be on an annual basis beginning January 1st of each year. Annual leave credits shall be based on time served by members during preceding calendar year. However, when credits have been accrued and member retires during current year, additional annual leave credits shall, in this instance, be granted at accrual rate of three days for each completed month of service, excluding terminal leave. If accruals granted for completed months of service extend into following month, member shall be granted an additional three days accrual for completed month. This shall be the only condition where accruals in a current year are granted for vacation period in such year.

1. According to the above paragraph, if a fireman's wife were to become seriously ill so that he would take time off from work to be with her, such time off would be deducted from his _____ allowance.

    A. annual leave   B. vacation leave
    C. personal business leave   D. family illness leave

1.____

2. Terminal leave means leave taken

    A. at the end of the calendar year
    B. at the end of the vacation year
    C. immediately before retirement
    D. before actually earned, because of an emergency

2.____

3. A fireman appointed on July 1, 2007 will be able to take his first full or normal annual leave during the period

    A. July 1, 2007 to June 30, 2008
    B. Jan. 1, 2008 to Dec. 31, 2008
    C. July 1, 2008 to June 30, 2009
    D. Jan. 1, 2009 to Dec. 31, 2009

3.____

4. According to the above paragraph, a member who retires on July 15 of this year will be   4.____
   entitled to receive leave allowance based on this year of _____ days.

   A. 15   B. 18   C. 22   D. 24

5. Fire alarm boxes are electromechanical devices for transmitting a coded signal. In each   5.____
   box, there is a trainwork of wheels. When the box is operated, a spring-activated code
   wheel within begins to revolve. The code number of the box is notched on the circumfer-
   ence of the code wheel, and the latter is associated with the circuit in such a way that
   when it revolves it causes the circuit to open and close in a predetermined manner,
   thereby transmitting its particular signal to the central station. A fire alarm box is nothing
   more than a device for interrupting the flow of current in a circuit in such a way as to produce a coded signal that may be decoded by the dispatchers in the central office.
   Based on the above, select the FALSE statement:

   A. Each standard fire alarm box has its own code wheel
   B. The code wheel operates when the box is pulled
   C. The code wheel is operated electrically
   D. Only the break in the circuit by the notched wheel causes the alarm signal to be
       transmitted to the central office

Questions 6-9.

DIRECTIONS: Questions 6 through 9 are to be answered SOLELY on the basis of the follow-
              ing paragraph.

   Ventilation, as used in fire fighting operations, means opening up a building or structure
in which a fire is burning to release the accumulated heat, smoke, and gases. Lack of knowledge of the principles of ventilation on the part of firemen may result in unnecessary punish-
ment due to ventilation being neglected or improperly handled. While ventilation itself
extinguishes no fires, when used in an intelligent manner, it allows firemen to get at the fire
more quickly, easily, and with less danger and hardship.

6. According to the above paragraph, the MOST important result of failure to apply the prin-   6.____
   ciples of ventilation at a fire may be

   A. loss of public confidence
   B. waste of water
   C. excessive use of equipment
   D. injury to firemen

7. It may be inferred from the above paragraph that the CHIEF advantage of ventilation is   7.____
   that it

   A. eliminates the need for gas masks
   B. reduces smoke damage
   C. permits firemen to work closer to the fire
   D. cools the fire

8. Knowledge of the principles of ventilation, as defined in the above paragraph, would be LEAST important in a fire in a   8.____

   A. tenement house
   B. grocery store
   C. ship's hold
   D. lumberyard

9. We may conclude from the above paragraph that for the well-trained and equipped fireman, ventilation is   9.____

   A. a simple matter
   B. rarely necessary
   C. relatively unimportant
   D. a basic tool

Questions 10-13.

DIRECTIONS: Questions 10 through 13 are to be answered SOLELY on the basis of the following passage.

Fire exit drills should be established and held periodically to effectively train personnel to leave their working area promptly upon proper signal and to evacuate the building, speedily but without confusion. All fire exit drills should be carefully planned and carried out in a serious manner under rigid discipline so as to provide positive protection in the event of a real emergency. As a general rule, the local fire department should be furnished advance information regarding the exact date and time the exit drill is scheduled. When it is impossible to hold regular drills, written instructions should be distributed to all employees.

Depending upon individual circumstances, fires in warehouses vary from those of fast development that are almost instantly beyond any possibility of employee control to others of relatively slow development where a small readily attackable flame may be present for periods of time up to 15 minutes or more during which simple attack with fire extinguishers or small building hoses may prevent the fire development. In any case, it is characteristic of many warehouse fires that at a certain point in development they flash up to the top of the stack, increase heat quickly, and spread rapidly. There is a degree of inherent danger in attacking warehouse type fires, and all employees should be thoroughly trained in the use of the types of extinguishers or small hoses in the buildings and well instructed in the necessity of always staying between the fire and a direct pass to an exit.

10. Employees should be instructed that, when fighting a fire, they MUST   10.____

   A. try to control the blaze
   B. extinguish any fire in 15 minutes
   C. remain between the fire and a direct passage to the exit
   D. keep the fire between themselves and the fire exit

11. Whenever conditions are such that regular fire drills cannot be held, then which one of the following actions should be taken?   11.____

   A. The local fire department should be notified.
   B. Rigid discipline should be maintained during work hours.
   C. Personnel should be instructed to leave their working area by whatever means are available.
   D. Employees should receive fire drill procedures in writing.

12. The above passage indicates that the purpose of fire exit drills is to train employees to   12.____

    A. control a fire before it becomes uncontrollable
    B. act as firefighters
    C. leave the working area promptly
    D. be serious

13. According to the above passage, fire exit drills will prove to be of UTMOST effectiveness   13.____
if

    A. employee participation is made voluntary
    B. they take place periodically
    C. the fire department actively participates
    D. they are held without advance planning

Questions 14-16.

DIRECTIONS: Questions 14 through 16 are to be answered SOLELY on the basis of the following paragraph.

    The heat output from unit heaters will depend on how fast and how completely dry hot steam fills the unit core. For complete and fast air removal and rapid drainage of condensate, use a trap actuated by water or vapor (inverted bucket trap) and not a trap operated by temperature only (thermostatic or bellows trap). A temperature-actuated trap will hold back the hot condensate until it cools to a point where the thermal element opens. When this happens, the condensate backs up in the heater and reduces the heat output. With a water-actuated trap, this will not happen as the water or condensate is discharged as fast as it is formed.

14. On the basis of the information given in the above paragraph, it can be concluded that   14.____
the PROPER type of trap to use for a unit heater is a(n) _____ trap.

    A. thermostatic   B. bellows-type
    C. inverted bucket   D. temperature

15. According to the above paragraph, the MAIN reason for using the type of trap specified   15.____
for a unit heater is to

    A. bring the condensate up to steam temperature
    B. prevent reduction in the heat output of the unit heater
    C. permit cycling of the heater
    D. maintain constant temperature of condensate in the trap

16. As used in the above paragraph, the word *actuated* means MOST NEARLY   16.____

    A. clogged   B. operated   C. cleaned   D. vented

Question 17 -25.

DIRECTIONS: Questions 17 through 25 are to be answered SOLELY on the basis of the following passage. Each question consists of a statement. You are to indicate whether the statement is TRUE (T) or FALSE (F).

MOVING AN OFFICE

An office with all its equipment is sometimes moved during working hours. This is a difficult task and must be done in an orderly manner to avoid confusion. The operation should be planned in such a way as not to interrupt the progress of work usually done in the office and to make possible the accurate placement of the furniture and records in the new location. If the office moves to a place inside the same building, the desks and files are moved with all their contents. If the movement is to another building, the contents of each desk and file are placed in boxes. Each box is marked with a letter showing the particular section in the new quarters to which it is to be moved. Also marked on each box is the number of the desk or file on which the box is to be placed. Each piece of equipment must have a numbered tag. The number of each piece of equipment is put in soft chalk on the floor in the new office to show the proper location, and several floor plans are made to show where each piece of equipment goes. When the moving is done, someone is stationed at each of the several exits of the old office to see that each box or piece of equipment has its destination clearly marked on it. At the new office, someone stands at each of the several entrances with a copy of the floor plan and directs the placing of the furniture and equipment according to the floor plan. No one should interfere at this point with the arrangements shown on the plan. Improvements in arrangement can be considered and made at a later date.

17. It is a hard job to move an office from one place to another during working hours.   17._____

18. Confusion cannot be avoided if an office is moved during working hours.   18._____

19. The work usually done in an office must be stopped for the day when the office is moved during working hours.   19._____

20. If an office is moved from one floor to another in the same building, the contents of a desk are taken out and put into boxes for moving.   20._____

21. If boxes are used to hold material from desks when moving an office, the box is numbered the same as the desk on which it is to be put.   21._____

22. Letters are marked in soft chalk on the floor at the new quarters to show where the desks should go when moved.   22._____

23. When the moving begins, a person is put at each exit of the old office to check that each box and piece of equipment has clearly marked on it where it to go.   23._____

24. A person stationed at each entrance of the new quarters to direct the placing of the furniture and equipment has a copy of the floor plan of the new quarters.   24._____

25. If, while the furniture is being moved into the new office, a person helping at a doorway gets an idea of a better way to arrange the furniture, he should change the planned arrangement and make a record of the change.   25._____

KEY (CORRECT ANSWERS)

1.	A		11.	D
2.	C		12.	C
3.	D		13.	B
4.	B		14.	C
5.	C		15.	B
6.	D		16.	B
7.	C		17.	T
8.	D		18.	F
9.	D		19.	F
10.	C		20.	F

21.	T
22.	F
23.	T
24.	T
25.	F

TEST 2

DIRECTIONS: Questions 1 through 4 are to be answered SOLELY on the basis of the following paragraph.

In all cases of homicide, members of the Police Department who investigate will make every effort to obtain statements from dying persons. Such statements are of the greatest importance to the District Attorney. In many cases, there may be a failure to solve the crime if they are not taken. The principal element to be considered in taking the declaration of a dying person is his mental attitude. In order to be admissible in evidence, the person must have no hope of recovery. The patient will be fully interrogated on that point before a statement is taken.

1.   In cases of homicide, according to the above paragraph, members of the police force will   1._____

    A.   try to change the mental attitude of the dying person
    B.   attempt to obtain a statement from the dying person
    C.   not give the information they obtain directly to the District Attorney
    D.   be careful not to injure the dying person unnecessarily

2.   The mental attitude of the person making the dying statement is of GREAT importance   2._____
because it can determine, according to the above paragraph, whether the

    A.   victim should be interrogated in the presence of witnesses
    B.   victim will be willing to make a statement of any kind
    C.   statement will tell the District Attorney who committed the crime
    D.   the statement can be used as evidence

3.   District Attorneys find that statements of a dying person are important, according to the   3._____
above paragraph, because

    A.   it may be that the victim will recover and then refuse to testify
    B.   they are important elements in determining the mental attitude of the victim
    C.   they present a point of view
    D.   it may be impossible to punish the criminal without such a statement

4.   A well-known gangster is found dying from a bullet wound. The patrolman first on the   4._____
scene, in the presence of witnesses, tells the man that he is going to die and asks, *Who shot you?* The gangster says, *Jones shot me, but he hasn't killed me. I'll live to get him.* He then falls back dead. According to the above paragraph, this statement is

    A.   *admissible* in evidence; the man was obviously speaking the truth
    B.   *not admissible* in evidence; the man obviously did not believe that he was dying
    C.   *admissible* in evidence; there were witnesses to the statement
    D.   *not admissible* in evidence; the victim did not sign any statement and the evidence is merely hearsay

Questions 5-7.

DIRECTIONS: Questions 5 through 7 are to be answered SOLELY on the basis of the following paragraph.

The factors contributing to crime and delinquency are varied and complex. The home and its immediate environment have been found to be crucial in determining the behavior patterns of the individual, and criminality can frequently be traced to faulty family relationships and a bad neighborhood. But in the search for a clearer understanding of the underlying causes of delinquent and criminal behavior, the total environment must be taken into consideration.

5. According to the above paragraph, family relationships   5.____

    A. tend to become faulty in bad neighborhoods
    B. are important in determining the actions of honest people as well as criminals
    C. are the only important element in the understanding of causes of delinquency
    D. are determined by the total environment

6. According to the above paragraph, the causes of crime and delinquency are   6.____

    A. not simple   B. not meaningless
    C. meaningless   D. simple

7. According to the above paragraph, faulty family relationships FREQUENTLY are   7.____

    A. responsible for varied and complex results
    B. caused when one or both parents have a criminal behavior pattern
    C. independent of the total environment
    D. the cause of criminal acts

Questions 8-10.

DIRECTIONS: Questions 8 through 10 are to be answered SOLELY on the basis of the following paragraph.

A change in the specific problems which confront the police and in the methods for dealing with them has taken place in the last few decades. The automobile is a two-way symbol of this change in policing. It menaces every city with a complicated traffic problem and has speeded up the process of committing a crime and making a getaway, but at the same time has increased the effectiveness of police operations. However, the major concern of police departments continues to be the antisocial or criminal actions and behavior of human beings.

8. On the basis of the above paragraph, it can be stated that, for the most part, in the past   8.____
few decades the specific problems of a police force

    A. have changed but the general problems have not
    B. as well as the general problems have changed
    C. have remained the same but the general problems have changed
    D. as well as the general problems have remained the same

9. According to the above paragraph, advances in science and industry have, in general,   9.____
made the police

    A. operations less effective from the overall point of view
    B. operations more effective from the overall point of view
    C. abandon older methods of solving police problems
    D. concern themselves more with the antisocial acts of human beings

10. The automobile is a *two-way symbol,* according to the above paragraph, because its use   10.____
    A. has speeded up getting to and away from the scene of a crime
    B. both helps and hurts police operations
    C. introduces a new antisocial act—traffic violation—and does away with criminals like horse thieves
    D. both increases and decreases speed by introducing traffic problems

Questions 11-14.

DIRECTIONS: Questions 11 through 14 are to be answered SOLELY on the basis of the following passage on INSTRUCTIONS TO COIN AND TOKEN CASHIERS.

INSTRUCTIONS TO COIN AND TOKEN CASHIERS

Cashiers should reset the machine registers to an even starting number before commencing the day's work. Money bags received directly from collecting agents shall be counted and receipted for on the collecting agent's form. Each cashier shall be responsible for all coin or token bags accepted by him. He must examine all bags to be used for bank deposits for cuts and holes before placing them in use. Care must be exercised so that bags are not cut in opening them. Each bag must be opened separately and verified before another bag is opened. The machine register must be cleared before starting the count of another bag. The amount shown on the machine register must be compared with the amount on the bag tag. The empty bag must be kept on the table for re-examination should there be a difference between the amount on the bag tag and the amount on the machine register.

11. A cashier should BEGIN his day's assignment by   11.____
    A. counting and accepting all money bags
    B. resetting the counting machine register
    C. examining all bags for cuts and holes
    D. verifying the contents of all money bags

12. In verifying the amount of money in the bags received from the collecting agent, it is BEST to   12.____
    A. check the amount in one bag at a time
    B. base the total on the amount on the collecting agent's form
    C. repeat the total shown on the bag tag
    D. refer to the bank deposit receipt

13. A cashier is instructed to keep each empty coin bag on his table while verifying its contents CHIEFLY because, long as the bag is on the table,   13.____
    A. it cannot be misplaced
    B. the supervisor can see how quickly the cashier works
    C. cuts and holes are easily noticed
    D. a recheck is possible in case the machine count disagrees with the bag tag total

14. The INSTRUCTIONS indicate that it is NOT proper procedure for a cashier to   14.____

A. assume that coin bags are free of cuts and holes
B. compare the machine register total with the total shown on the bag tag
C. sign a form when he receives coin bags
D. reset the machine register before starting the day's counting

Questions 15-17.

DIRECTIONS: Questions 15 through 17 are to be answered SOLELY on the basis of the following passage.

The mass media are an integral part of the daily life of virtually every American. Among
these media the youngest, television, is the most pervasive. Ninety-five percent of American
homes have at least one T.V. set, and on the average that set is in use for about 40 hours
each week. The central place of television in American life makes this medium the focal point
of a growing national concern over the effects of media portrayals of violence on the values,
attitudes, and behavior of an ever increasing audience.

In our concern about violence and its causes, it is easy to make television a scapegoat.
But we emphasize the fact that there is no simple answer to the problem of violence—no single explanation of its causes, and no single prescription for its control. It should be remem-
bered that America also experienced high levels of crime and violence in periods before the
advent of television.

The problem of balance, taste, and artistic merit in entertaining programs on television
are complex. We cannot countenance government censorship of television. Nor would we
seek to impose arbitrary limitations on programming which might jeopardize television's ability to deal in dramatic presentations with controversial social issues. Nonetheless, we are
deeply troubled by television's constant portrayal of violence, not in any genuine attempt to
focus artistic expression on the human condition, but rather in pandering to a public preoccu-
pation with violence that television itself has helped to generate.

15. According to the above passage, television uses violence MAINLY   15.____

A. to highlight the reality of everyday existence
B. to satisfy the audience's hunger for destructive action
C. to shape the values and attitudes of the public
D. when it films documentaries concerning human conflict

16. Which one of the following statements is BEST supported by the above passage?   16.____

A. Early American history reveals a crime pattern which is not related to television.
B. Programs should give presentations of social issues and never portray violent acts.
C. Television has proven that entertainment programs can easily make the balance
between taste and artistic merit a simple matter.
D. Values and behavior should be regulated by governmental censorship.

17. Of the following, which word has the same meaning as countenance, as used in the   17.____
above passage?

A. Approve   B. Exhibit   C. Oppose   D. Reject

DIRECTIONS: Questions 18 through 21 are to be answered SOLELY on the basis of the following passage.

Maintenance of leased or licensed areas on public parks or lands has always been a problem. A good rule to follow in the administration and maintenance of such areas is to limit the responsibility of any lessee or licensee to the maintenance of the structures and grounds essential to the efficient operation of the concession, not including areas for the general use of the public, such as picnic areas, public comfort stations, etc.; except where such facilities are leased to another public agency or where special conditions make such inclusion practicable, and where a good standard of maintenance can be assured and enforced. If local conditions and requirements are such that public use areas are included, adequate safeguards to the public should be written into contracts and enforced in their administration, to insure that maintenance by the concessionaire shall be equal to the maintenance standards for other park property.

18. According to the above passage, when an area on a public park is leased to a concessionaire, it is usually BEST to

    A. confine the responsibility of the concessionaire to operation of the facilities and leave the maintenance function to the park agency
    B. exclude areas of general public use from the maintenance obligation of the concessionaire
    C. make the concessionaire responsible for maintenance of the entire area including areas of general public use
    D. provide additional comfort station facilities for the area

18.____

19. According to the above passage, a valid reason for giving a concessionaire responsibility for maintenance of a picnic area within his leased area is that

    A. local conditions and requirements make it practicable
    B. more than half of the picnic area falls within his leased area
    C. the concessionaire has leased picnic facilities to another public agency
    D. the picnic area falls entirely within his leased area

19.____

20. According to the above passage, a precaution that should be taken when a concessionaire is made responsible for maintenance of an area of general public use in a park is

    A. making sure that another public agency has not previously been made responsible for this area
    B. providing the concessionaire with up-to-date equipment, if practicable
    C. requiring that the concessionaire take out adequate insurance for the protection of the public
    D. writing safeguards to the public into the contract

20.____

KEY (CORRECT ANSWERS)

1.	B		11.	B
2.	D		12.	A
3.	D		13.	D
4.	B		14.	A
5.	B		15.	B
6.	A		16.	A
7.	D		17.	A
8.	A		18.	B
9.	B		19.	A
10.	B		20.	D

———

TEST 3

DIRECTIONS: Questions 1 through 5 are to be answered SOLELY on the basis of the following paragraph.

Physical inspections are an important tool for the examiner because he will have to
decide the case in many instances on the basis of the inspection report. Most proceedings in
a rent office are commenced by the filing of a written application or complaint by an interested
party; that is, either the landlord or the tenant. Such an application or complaint must be filed
in duplicate in order that the opposing party may be served with a copy of the application or
complaint and thus be given an opportunity to answer and oppose it. Sometimes, a further
opportunity is given the applicant to file a written rebuttal or reply to his adversary's answer.
Often an examiner can make a determination or decision based on the written application,
the answer, and the reply to the answer; and, of course, it would speed up operations if it
were always possible to make decisions based on written documents only. Unfortunately,
decisions can't always be made that way. There are numerous occasions where <u>disputed</u>
issues of fact remain which cannot be <u>resolved</u> on the basis of the written statements of the
parties. Typical examples are the following: The tenant claims that the refrigerator or stove or
bathroom fixture is not functioning properly and the landlord denies this. It is obvious that in
such cases an inspection of the accommodations is almost the only means of resolving such
disputed issues.

1. According to the above paragraph,   1._____

    A. physical inspections are made in all cases
    B. physical inspections are seldom made
    C. it is sometimes possible to determine the facts in a case without a physical inspec-
        tion
    D. physical inspections are made when it is necessary to verify the examiner's deter-
        mination

2. According to the above paragraph, in MOST cases, proceedings are started by a(n)   2._____

    A. inspector discovering a violation
    B. oral complaint by a tenant or landlord
    C. request from another agency, such as the Building Department
    D. written complaint by a tenant or landlord

3. According to the above paragraph, when a tenant files an application with the rent office,   3._____
    the landlord is

    A. not told about the proceeding until after the examiner makes his determination
    B. given the duplicate copy of the application
    C. notified by means of an inspector visiting the premises
    D. not told about the proceeding until after the inspector has visited the Premises

4. As used in the above paragraph, the word *disputed* means MOST NEARLY   4._____

    A. unsettled   B. contested
    C. definite   D. difficult

5. As used in the above paragraph, the word *resolved* means MOST NEARLY   5._____

   A. settled   B. fixed   C. helped   D. amended

Questions 6-10.

DIRECTIONS: Questions 6 through 10 are to be answered SOLELY on the basis of the follow-
              ing paragraph.

The examiner should order or request an inspection of the housing accommodations. His
request for a physical inspection should be in writing, identify the accommodations and the
landlord and the tenant, and specify <u>precisely</u> just what the inspector is to look for and report
on. Unless this request is specific and lists <u>in detail</u> every item which the examiner wishes to
be reported, the examiner will find that the inspection has not served its purpose and that
even with the inspector's report, he is still in no position to decide the case due to loose ends
which have not been completely tied up. The items that the examiner is interested in should
be separately numbered on the inspection request and the same number referred to in the
inspector's report. You can see what it would mean if an inspector came back with a report
that did not cover everything. It may mean a tremendous waste of time and often require a re-
inspection.

6. According to the above paragraph, the inspector makes an inspection on the order of   6._____

   A. the landlord
   B. the tenant
   C. the examiner
   D. both the landlord and the tenant

7. According to the above paragraph, the reason for numbering each item that an inspector   7._____
   reports on is so that

   A. the report is neat
   B. the report can be easily read and referred to
   C. none of the examiner's requests for information is missed
   D. the report will be specific

8. The one of the following items that is NOT necessarily included in the request for inspec-   8._____
   tion is

   A. location of dwelling   B. name of landlord
   C. item to be checked   D. type of building

9. As used in the above paragraph, the word precisely means MOST NEARLY   9._____

   A. exactly   B. generally   C. Usually   D. strongly

10. As used in the above paragraph, the words in detail mean MOST NEARLY   10._____

   A. clearly   B. item by item
   C. substantially   D. completely

Questions 11-13.

DIRECTIONS: Questions 11 through 13 are to be answered SOLELY on the basis of the following passage.

The agreement under which a tenant rents property from a landlord is known as a lease. Generally speaking, leases are classified as either short-term or long-term in duration. They are further subdivided according to the method used to determine the amount of periodic rent payments. Of the following types of lease in use, the more commonly used ones are the following:

1. The straight or fixed lease is one in which rent may be paid in equal amounts throughout the duration of the lease. These are usually restricted to short-term leasing, or somewhat longer-term if clauses in the lease provide for periodic escalation of payments as the economy shifts.

2. Percentage leasing, used for short-term commercial leasing, provides the landlord with a stipulated percentage of a tenant's gross sales from goods and services sold on the premises, in addition to a fixed amount of rent.

3. The net lease, generally long-term (ten years or more), requires the tenant to pay all operating costs, including real estate taxes and insurance. In a net-net lease, the tenant further agrees to meet mortgage interest and principal payments.

4. An escalated lease, which is a long-term lease, requires rent to be of a stipulated base amount which periodically is subject to escalation in accordance with cost-of-living index scales, or in direct proportion to taxes, insurance, and operating costs.

11. Based on the information given in the passage, which type of lease is MOST likely to be advantageous to a landlord if there is a high rate of inflation? _____ lease.   11.____

    A. Fixed   B. Percentage   C. Net   D. Escalated

12. On the basis of the above passage, which types of lease would generally be MOST suitable for a well-established textile company which requires permanent facilities for its large operations?   12.____
    _____ lease and _____ lease.

    A. Percentage; escalated   B. Escalated; net
    C. Straight; net   D. Straight; percentage

13. According to the above passage, the ONLY type of lease which assures the same amount of rent throughout a specified interval is the _____ lease.   13.____

    A. straight   B. percentage   C. net-net   D. escalated

Questions 14-15.

DIRECTIONS: Questions 14 and 15 are to be answered SOLELY on the basis of the following passage.

If you like people, if you seek contact with them rather than hide yourself in a corner, if you study your fellow men sympathetically, if you try consistently to contribute something to their success and happiness, if you are reasonably generous with your thought and your time, if you have a partial reserve with everyone but a seeming reserve with no one, you will get along with your superiors, your subordinates, and the human race.

By the scores of thousands, precepts and platitudes have been written for the guidance of personal conduct. The odd part of it is that, despite all of this labor, most of the frictions in modern society arise from the individual's feeling of inferiority, his false pride, his vanity, his unwillingness to yield space to any other man and his consequent urge to throw his own weight around. Goethe said that the quality which best enables a man to renew his own life, in his relation to others, is his capability of renouncing particular things at the right moment in order warmly to embrace something new in the next.

14. On the basis of the above passage, it may be INFERRED that   14.____

    A. a person should be unwilling to renounce privileges
    B. a person should realize that loss of a desirable job assignment may come at an opportune moment
    C. it is advisable for a person to maintain a considerable amount of reserve in his relationship with unfamiliar people
    D. people should be ready to contribute generously to a worthy charity

15. Of the following, the MOST valid implication made by the above passage is that   15.____

    A. a wealthy person who spends a considerable amount of money entertaining his friends is not really getting along with them
    B. if a person studies his fellow men carefully and impartially, he will tend to have good relationships with them
    C. individuals who maintain seemingly little reserve in their relationships with people have in some measure overcome their own feelings of inferiority
    D. most precepts that have been written for the guidance of personal conduct in relationships with other people are invalid

Questions 16-17.

DIRECTIONS: Questions 16 and 17 are to be answered SOLELY on the basis of the following passage.

When a design for a new bank note of the Federal Government has been prepared by the Bureau of Engraving and Printing and has been approved by the Secretary of the Treasury, the engravers begin the work of cutting the design in steel. No one engraver does all the work. Each man is a specialist. One works only on portraits, another on lettering, another on scroll work, and so on. Each engraver, with a steel tool known as a graver, and aided by a powerful magnifying glass, carefully carves his portion of the design into the steel. He knows that one false cut or a slip of his tool, or one miscalculation of width or depth of line, may destroy the merit of his work. A single mistake means that months or weeks of labor will have been in vain. The Bureau is proud of the fact that no counterfeiter ever has duplicated the excellent work of its expert engravers.

16. According to the above passage, each engraver in the Bureau of Engraving and Printing   16.____

    A. must be approved by the Secretary of the Treasury before he can begin work on the design for a new bank note
    B. is responsible for engraving a complete design of a new bank note by himself
    C. designs new bank notes and submits them for approval to the Secretary of the Treasury
    D. performs only a specific part of the work of engraving a design for a new bank note

17. According to the above passage,

    A. an engraver's tools are not available to a counterfeiter
    B. mistakes made in engraving a design can be corrected immediately with little delay in the work of the Bureau
    C. the skilled work of the engravers has not been successfully reproduced by counterfeiter
    D. careful carving and cutting by the engravers is essential to prevent damage to equipment

17.____

Questions 18-21.

DIRECTIONS: Questions 18 through 21 are to be answered SOLELY on the basis of the following passage.

    In the late fifties, the average American housewife spent $4.50 per day for a family of four on food and 5.15 hours in food preparation, if all of her food was *home prepared;* she spent $5.80 per day and 3.25 hours if all of her food was purchased *partially prepared;* and $6.70 per day and 1.65 hours if all of her food was purchased *ready to serve.*

    Americans spent about 20 billion dollars for food products in 1941. They spent nearly 70 billion dollars in 1958. They spent 25 percent of their cash income on food in 1958. For the same kinds and quantities of food that consumers bought in 1941, they would have spent only 16% of their cash income in 1958. It is obvious that our food does cost more. Many factors contribute to this increase besides the additional cost that might be attributed to processing. Consumption of more expensive food items, higher marketing margins, and more food eaten in restaurants are other factors.

    The Census of Manufacturers gives some indication of the total bill for processing. The value added by manufacturing of food and kindred products amounted to 3.5 billion of the 20 billion dollars spent for food in 1941. In the year 1958, the comparable figure had climbed to 14 billion dollars.

18. According to the above passage, the cash income of Americans in 1958 was MOST NEARLY _____ billion dollars.

    A. 11.2   B. 17.5   C. 70   D. 280

18.____

19. According to the above passage, if Americans bought the same kinds and quantities of food in 1958 as they did in 1941, they would have spent MOST NEARLY _____ billion dollars.

    A. 20   B. 45   C. 74   D. 84

19.____

20. According to the above passage, the percent increase in money spent for food in 1958 over 1941, as compared with the percentage increase in money spent for food processing in the same years,

    A. was greater
    B. was less
    C. was the same
    D. cannot be determined from the passage

20.____

21. In 1958, an American housewife who bought all of her food ready-to-serve saved in time,   21.____
    as compared with the housewife who prepared all of her food at home

    A. 1.6 hours daily
    B. 1.9 hours daily
    C. 3.5 hours daily
    D. an amount of time which cannot be determined from the above passage

Questions 22-25.

DIRECTIONS: Questions 22 through 25 are to be answered SOLELY on the basis of the fol-
              lowing passage.

Any member of the retirement system who is in city service, who files a proper application for service credit and agrees to deductions from his compensation at triple his normal
rate of contribution, shall be credited with a period of city service previous to the beginning of
his present membership in the retirement system. The period of service credited shall be
equal to the period throughout which such triple deductions are made, but may not exceed
the total of the city service the member rendered between his first day of eligibility for membership in the retirement system and the day he last became a member. After triple contributions for all of the first three years of service credit claimed, the remaining service credit may
be purchased by a single payment of the sum of the remaining payments. If the total time pur-
chasable exceeds ten years, triple contributions may be made for one-half of such time, and
the remaining time purchased by a single payment of the sum of the remaining payments.
Credit for service acquired in the above manner may be used only in determining the amount
of any retirement benefit. Eligibility for such benefit will, in all cases, be based upon service
rendered after the employee's membership last began, and will be exclusive of service credit
purchased as described below.

22. According to the above passage, in order to obtain credit for city service previous to the   22.____
    beginning of an employee's present membership in the retirement system, the employee
    must

    A. apply for the service credit and consent to additional contributions to the retirement
       system
    B. apply for the service credit before he renews his membership in the retirement sys-
       tem
    C. have previous city service which does not exceed ten years
    D. make contributions to the retirement system for three years

23. According to the information in the above passage, credit for city service previous to the   23.____
    beginning of an employee's present membership in the retirement system, is

    A. credited up to a maximum of ten years
    B. credited to any member of the retirement system
    C. used in determining the amount of the employee's benefits
    D. used in establishing the employee's eligibility to receive benefits

24. According to the information in the above passage, a member of the retirement system may purchase service credit for   24.____

    A.   the period of time between his first day of eligibility for membership in the retirement system and the date he applies for the service credit
    B.   one-half of the total of his previous city service if the total time exceeds ten years
    C.   the period of time throughout which triple deductions are made
    D.   the period of city service between his first day of eligibility for membership in the retirement system and the day he last became a member

25. Suppose that a member of the retirement system has filed an application for service credit for five years of previous city service.   25.____
Based on the information in the above passage, the employee may purchase credit for this previous city service by making

    A.   triple contributions for three years
    B.   triple contributions for one-half of the time and a single payment of the sum of the remaining payments
    C.   triple contributions for three years and a single payment of the sum of the remaining payments
    D.   a single payment of the sum of the payments

KEY (CORRECT ANSWERS)

1.	C		11.	D
2.	D		12.	B
3.	B		13.	A
4.	B		14.	B
5.	A		15.	C
6.	C		16.	D
7.	C		17.	C
8.	D		18.	D
9.	A		19.	B
10.	B		20.	B

21.	C
22.	A
23.	C
24.	D
25.	C

NUMBER SERIES PROBLEMS
COMMENTARY

Number series problems constitute an important means for measuring quantitative ability on the part of applicants for beginning and trainee positions as well as for regular, mid-level, and senior level positions.

In this method, numerical reasoning forms the primary technic for measuring mathematic -cal ability.

This test measures your ability to think with numbers instead of words.

In each problem, you are given a series of numbers that are changing according to a rule - followed by five sets of 2 numbers each. Your problem is to figure out a rule that would make one of the five sets the next two numbers in the series.

The problems do not use hard arithmetic. The task is merely to see how the numbers are related to each other. The sample questions will explain several types in detail so that you may become familiar with what you have to do.

HINTS FOR ANSWERING NUMBER SERIES QUESTIONS

1. Do the ones that are easier for you *first.* Then go back and work on the others. Enough time is allowed for you to do all the questions, provided you don't stay too long on the ones you have trouble answering.
2. Sound out the series to yourself. You may hear the rule: 2468 10 12 14 ... What are the next two numbers?
3. Look at the series carefully. You may see the rule: 9294969... What are the next two numbers?
4. If you can't hear it or see it, you may have to figure it out by writing down how the numbers are changing: 6 8 16 18 26 28 36 ... What are the next two numbers?
   $6^{+2} 8^{+8} 16^{+2} 18^{+8} 26^{+2} 28^{+8} 36...$. What are the next two numbers if this is +2 +8? 36 + 2 = 38 + 8 = 46 or 38 46. You would mark the letter of the answer that goes with 38 46.
5. If none of the answers given fits the rule you have figured out, try again. Try to figure out a rule that makes one of the five answers a correct one.
6. Don't spend too much time on any one question. Skip it and come back. A fresh look sometimes helps.

SAMPLE QUESTIONS

DIRECTIONS: In each of the questions in this test, there is at the top a series of numbers which follow some definite order and, below, five sets of two numbers each. You are to look at the numbers in the series at the top and find out what order they follow. Then decide what the next two numbers in that series would be if the same order were continued. Next find these two numbers in one of the sets below. *PRINT THE LETTER OF THE CORRECT ANSWER IN THE SPACE AT THE RIGHT.*

1. 1 2 3 4 5 6 7 .....   1.____

   A. 1 2   B. 5 6   C. 8 9   D. 4 5   E. 7 8

   How are these numbers changing? The numbers in this series are increasing by 1 or the rule is "add 1." If you apply this rule to the series, what would the next two numbers be? 7+1=8+1=9.
   Therefore, the CORRECT answer is 8 and 9, and you would select C. 8 9 as your answer.

2. 15 14 13 12 11 10 9 ....   2.____

   A. 2 1   B. 17 16   C. 8 9   D. 8 7   E. 9 8

   The numbers in this series are decreasing by 1 or the rule is "subtract 1." If you apply that rule, what would the next two numbers be? 9-1=8-1=7. The CORRECT answer is 8 and 7, and you would select D. 8 7 as your answer.

3. 20 20 21 21 22 22 23 ....   3.____

   A. 23 23   B. 23 24   C. 19 19   D. 22 23   E. 21 22

   In this series each number is repeated and then increased by 1. The rule is "repeat , add 1. repeat, add 1, etc." The series would be $20^{+0}20^{+1}21^{+0}21^{+1}22^{+0}22^{+1}23^{+0}23^{+1}24$. The CORRECT answer is 23 and 24, and you should have selected B. 23 24 as your answer.

4. 17 3 17 4 17 5 17 ....   4.____

   A. 6 17   B. 6 7   C. 17 6   D. 5 6   E. 17 7

   If you can't find a single rule for all the numbers in a series, see if there are really two series in the problem. This series is the number 17 separated by numbers increasing by 1, starting with 3. If the series were continued for two more numbers, it would read 17 3 17 4 17 5 17 6 17. The CORRECT answer is 6 and 17, and you should have selected A. 6 17 for question 4.

5. 1 2 4 5 7 8 10 ....   5.____

   A. 11 12   B. 12 14   C. 10 13   D. 12 13   E. 11 13

   The rule in this series is not easy to see until you actually set down how the numbers are changing: $I^{+1}2^{+2}4^{+1}5^{+2}7^{+1}8^{+2}10$. The numbers in this series are increasing first by 1 (that is, plus 1) and then by 2 (that is, plus 2). If the series were continued for two more numbers, it would read: 1 2 4 5 7 8 10 (plus 1) which is 11 (plus 2) which is 13. Therefore, the CORRECT answer is 11 and 13, and you should have selected E. 11 13 for question 5.

NOW READ AND WORK SAMPLE QUESTIONS 6 THROUGH 10 AND MARK FOUR ANSWERS IN THE SPACE PROVIDED AT THE RIGHT.

6. 21 21 20 20 19 19 18 ....   6._____

    A. 18 18   B. 18 17   C. 17 18   D. 17 17   E. 18 19

7. 1 22 1 23 1 24 1 ....   7._____

    A. 2 61   B. 25 26   C. 2 51   D. 1 26   E. 1 25

8. 1 20 3 19 5 18 7 ....   8._____

    A. 8 9   B. 8 17   C. 17 10   D. 17 9   E. 9 18

9. 4 7 10 13 16 19 22 ...   9._____

    A. 23 26   B. 25 27   C. 25 26   D. 25 28   E. 24 27

10. 30 2 28 4 26 6 24 ....   10._____

    A. 23 9   B. 26 8   C. 8 9   D. 26 22   E. 8 22

EXPLANATIONS FOR QUESTIONS 6 THROUGH 10.

6. Each number in the series repeats itself and then decreases by 1 or minus 1; 21 (repeat) 21 (minus 1) which makes 20 (repeat) 20 (minus 1) which makes 19 (repeat) 19 (minus 1) which makes 18 (repeat) ? (minus 1) ? The CORRECT answer is B.

7. The number 1 is separated by numbers which begin with 22 and increase by 1; 1 22 1 (increase 22 by 1) which makes 23 1 (increase 23 by 1) which makes 24 1 (increase 24 by 1) which makes ? The CORRECT answer is C.

8. This is best explained by two alternating series - one series starts with 1 and increases by 2 or plus 2; the other series starts with 20 and decreases by 1 or minus 1. The CORRECT answer is D.

$$1\uparrow3\uparrow5\uparrow7\uparrow?$$

9. This series of numbers increases by 3 (plus 3) beginning with the first number - 4 (plus 3) 7 (plus 3) 10 (plus 3) 13 (plus 3) 16 (plus 3) 19 (plus 3) 22 (plus 3) ? The CORRECT answer is D.

10. Look for two alternating series - one series starts with 30 and decreases by 2 (minus 2); the other series starts with 2 and increases by 2 (plus 2). The CORRECT answer is E.

$$30\uparrow28\uparrow26\uparrow24\uparrow?$$
$$2\quad4\quad6\quad7$$

KEY (CORRECT ANSWERS)

1.	C	6.	B
2.	D	7.	C
3.	B	8.	D
4.	A	9.	D
5.	E	10.	E

NUMBER SERIES PROBLEMS
EXAMINATION SECTION
TEST 1

DIRECTIONS : In each of the questions in this test, there is at the top a series of numbers which follow some definite order and, below, five sets of two numbers each. You are to look at the numbers in the series at the top and find out what order they follow. Then decide what the next two numbers in that series would be if the same order were continued. Next find these two numbers in one of the sets below. *PRINT THE LETTER OF THE CORRECT ANSWER IN THE SPACE AT THE RIGHT.*

1.   5 6 20 7 8 19 9 ....   1._____
   A.   10 18   B.   18 17   C.   10 17   D.   18 19   E.   10 11

2.   9 10 1 11 12 2 13 ....   2._____
   A.   2 14   B.   3 14   C.   14 3   D.   14 15   E.   14 1

3.   4 6 9 11 14 16 19 ....   3._____
   A.   21 24   B.   22 25   C.   20 22   D.   21 23   E.   22 24

4.   8 8 1 10 10 3 12 ....   4._____
   A.   13 13   B.   12 5   C.   12 4   D.   13 5   E.   4 12

5.   14 1 2 15 3 4 16 ....   5._____
   A.   5 16   B.   6 7   C.   5 17   D.   5 6   E.   17 5

6.   10 12 50 15 17 50 20 ....   6._____
   A.   50 21   B.   21 50   C.   50 22   D.   22 50   E.   22 24

7.   1 2 3 50 4 5 6 51 7 8 ....   7._____
   A.   9 10   B.   9 52   C.   51 10   D.   10 52   E.   10 50

8.   20 21 23 24 27 28 32 33 38 39 ....   8._____
   A.   45 46   B.   45 52   C.   44 45   D.   44 49   E.   40 46

9.   17 15 21 18 10 16 19 ....   9._____
   A.   20 5   B.   5 11   C.   11 11   D.   11 20   E.   15 14

10. 12 16 10 14 8 12 6 ....   10._____
   A.   10 14   B.   10 8   C.   10 4   D.   4 10   E.   4 2

KEY (CORRECT ANSWERS)

1.	A		6.	D
2.	C		7.	B
3.	A		8.	A
4.	B		9.	B
5.	D		10.	C

TEST 2

DIRECTIONS : In each of the questions in this test, there is at the top a series of numbers which follow some definite order and, below, five sets of two numbers each. You are to look at the numbers in the series at the top and find out what order they follow. Then decide what the next two numbers in that series would be if the same order were continued. Next find these two numbers in one of the sets below. *PRINT THE LETTER OF THE CORRECT ANSWER IN THE SPACE AT THE RIGHT.*

1. 10 11 12 10 11 12 10 ....   1.____
   A. 10 13   B. 12 10   C. 11 10   D. 11 12   E. 10 12

2. 4 6 7 4 6 7 4   2.____
   A. .6 7   B. 4 7   C. 7 6   D. 7 4   E. 6 8

3. 7 7 3 7 7 4 7....   3.____
   A. 4 5   B. 4 7   C. 5 7   D. 7 5   E. 7 7

4. 3 4 10 5 6 10 7 ....   4.____
   A. 10 8   B. 9 8   C. 8 14   D. 8 9   E. 8 10

5. 6 6 7 7 8 8 9 ....   5.____
   A. 10 11   B. 10 10   C. 9 10   D. 9 9   E. 10 9

6. 3 8 9 4 9 10 5 ....   6.____
   A. 6 10   B. 10 11   C. 9 10   D. 11 6   E. 10 6

7. 2 4 3 6 4 8 5....   7.____
   A. 6 10   B. 10 7   C. 10 6   D. 9 6   E. 6 7

8. 11 5 9 7 7 9 5 ....   8.____
   A. 11 3   B. 7 9   C. 7 11   D. 9 7   E. 3 7

9. 12 10 8 8 6 4 4 ....   9.____
   A. 2 2   B. 6 4   C. 6 2   D. 4 6   E. 2 0

10. 20 22 22 19 21 21 18 ....   10.____
    A. 22 22   B. 19 19   C. 20 20   D. 20 17   E. 19 17

KEY (CORRECT ANSWERS)

1. D	6. B
2. A	7. C
3. D	8. A
4. E	9. E
5. C	10. C

TEST 3

DIRECTIONS : In each of the questions in this test, there is at the top a series of numbers which follow some definite order and, below, five sets of two numbers each. You are to look at the numbers in the series at the top and find out what order they follow. Then decide what the next two numbers in that series would be if the same order were continued. Next find these two numbers in one of the sets below. *PRINT THE LETTER OF THE CORRECT ANSWER IN THE SPACE AT THE RIGHT.*

1. 5 7 6 10 7 13 8 ....

   A. 16 9   B. 16 10   C. 9 15   D. 10 15   E. 15 9

   1.____

2. 13 10 11 15 12 13 17 ....

   A. 18 14   B. 18 15   C. 15 16   D. 14 15   E. 15 18

   2.____

3. 30 27 24 21 18 15 12 ....

   A. 9 3   B. 9 6   C. 6 3   D. 12 9   E. 8 5

   3.____

4. 3 7 10 5 8 10 7 ....

   A. 10 11   B. 10 5   C. 10 9   D. 10 10   E. 9 10

   4.____

5. 12 4 13 6 14 8 15 ....

   A. 10 17   B. 17 10   C. 10 12   D. 16 10   E. 10 16

   5.____

6. 21 8 18 20 7 17 19 ....

   A. 16 18   B. 18. 6   C. 6 16   D. 5 15   E. 6 18

   6.____

7. 14 16 16 18 20 20 22 ....

   A. 22 24   B. 26 28   C. 24 26   D. 24 24   E. 24 28

   7.____

8. 5 6 8 9 12 13 17 ....

   A. 18 23   B. 13 18   C. 18 22   D. 23 24   E. 18 19

   8.____

9. 1 3 5 5 2 4 6 6 3 ....

   A. 7 4   B. 5 5   C. 1 3   D. 5 7   E. 7 7

   9.____

10. 12 24 15 25 18 26 21 ....

    A. 27 22   B. 24 22   C. 29 24   D. 27 27   E. 27 24

    10.____

KEY (CORRECT ANSWERS)

1.	A	6.	C
2.	D	7.	D
3.	B	8.	A
4.	E	9.	D
5.	E	10.	E

TEST 4

DIRECTIONS : In each of the questions in this test, there is at the top a series of numbers which follow some definite order and, below, five sets of two numbers each. You are to look at the numbers in the series at the top and find out what order they follow. Then decide what the next two numbers in that series would be if the same order were continued. Next find these two numbers in one of the sets below. *PRINT THE LETTER OF THE CORRECT ANSWER IN THE SPACE AT THE RIGHT.*

1. 8 9 9 8 10 10 8 ....

    A. 11 8   B. 8 13   C. 8 11   D. 11 11   E. 8 8   1.____

2. 10 10 11 11 12 12 13 ....

    A. 15 15   B. 13 13   C. 14 14   D. 13 14   E. 14 15   2.____

3. 6 6 10 6 6 12 6 ....

    A. 6 14   B. 13 6   C. 14 6   D. 6 13   E. 6 6   3.____

4. 17 11 5 16 10 4 15 ....

    A. 13 9   B. 13 11   C. 8 5   D. 9 5   E. 9 3   4.____

5. 1 3 2 4 3 5 4....

    A. 6 8   B. 5 6   C. 6 5   D. 3 4   E. 3 5   5.____

6. 11 11 10 12 12 11 13 ....

    A. 12 14   B. 14 12   C. 14 14   D. 13 14   E. 13 12   6.____

7. 18 5 6 18 7 8 18 ....

    A. 9 9   B. 9 10   C. 18 9   D. 8 9   E. 18 7   7.____

8. 7 8 9 13 10 11 12 14 13 14 ....

    A. 15 16   B. 13 15   C. 14 15   D. 15 15   E. 13 14   8.____

9. 5 7 30 9 11 30 13 ....

    A. 15 16   B. 15 17   C. 14 17   D. 15 30   E. 30 17   9.____

10. 5 7 11 13 17 19 23 ....

    A. 27 29   B. 25 29   C. 25 27   D. 27 31   E. 29 31   10.____

KEY (CORRECT ANSWERS)

1.	D	6.	E
2.	D	7.	B
3.	A	8.	D
4.	E	9.	D
5.	C	10.	B

8

TEST 5

DIRECTIONS : In each of the questions in this test, there is at the top a series of numbers which follow some definite order and, below, five sets of two numbers each. You are to look at the numbers in the series at the top and find out what order they follow. Then decide what the next two numbers in that series would be if the same order were continued. Next find these two numbers in one of the sets below. *PRINT THE LETTER OF THE CORRECT ANSWER IN THE SPACE AT THE RIGHT.*

1. 9 15 10 17 12 19 15 21 19....
   A. 23 24   B. 25 23   C. 17 23   D. 23 31   E. 21 24   1._____

2. 34 37 30 33 26 29 22 ....
   A. 17 8   B. 18 11   C. 25 28   D. 25 20   E. 25 18   2._____

3. 10 16 12 14 14 12 16 ....
   A. 14 12   B. 10 18   C. 10 14   D. 14 18   E. 14 16   3._____

4. 11 12 18 11 13 19 11 14 ....
   A. 18 11   B. 16 11   C. 20 11   D. 11 21   E. 17 11   4._____

5. 20 9 8 19 10 9 18 11 10 ....
   A. 19 11   B. 17 10   C. 19 12   D. 17 12   E. 19 10   5._____

6. 28 27 26 31 30 29 34 ....
   A. 36 32   B. 32 31   C. 33 32   D. 33 36   E. 35 36   6._____

7. 10 16 14 20 18 24 22 ....
   A. 28 32   B. 27 26   C. 28 26   D. 26 28   E. 27 28   7._____

8. 9 9 7 8 7 7 9 10 5 ....
   A. 5 11   B. 11 12   C. 5 9   D. 9 11   E. 5 5   8._____

9. 5 7 11 17 10 12 16 22 15 17 ....
   A. 27 26   B. 19 23   C. 19 27   D. 21 23   E. 21 27   9._____

10. 12 19 13 20 14 21 15 ....
   A. 16 17   B. 22 16   C. 16 22   D. 15 22   E. 15 16   10._____

KEY (CORRECT ANSWERS)

6.	A	11.	C
7.	E	12.	C
8.	B	13.	A
9.	C	14.	E
10.	D	15.	B

118

TEST 6

DIRECTIONS : In each of the questions in this test, there is at the top a series of numbers which follow some definite order and, below, five sets of two numbers each. You are to look at the numbers in the series at the top and find out what order they follow. Then decide what the next two numbers in that series would be if the same order were continued. Next find these two numbers in one of the sets below. *PRINT THE LETTER OF THE CORRECT ANSWER IN THE SPACE AT THE RIGHT.*

1. 13 12 8 11 10 8 9 ....   1.____
    A. 8 7   B. 6 8   C. 8 6   D. 8 8   E. 7 8

2. 13 18 13 17 13 16 13 ....   2.____
    A. 15 13   B. 13 14   C. 13 15   D. 14 15   E. 15 14

3. 13 13 10 12 12 10 11 ....   3.____
    A. 10 10   B. 10 9   C. 11 9   D. 9 11   E. 11 10

4. 6 5 4 6 5 4 6....   4.____
    A. 4 6   B. 6 4   C. 5 4   D. 5 6   E. 4 5

5. 10 10 9 8 8 7 6 ....   5.____
    A. 5 5   B. 5 4   C. 6 5   D. 6 4   E. 5 3

6. 20 16 18 14 16 12 14 ....   6.____
    A. 16 12   B. 10 12   C. 16 18   D. 12 12   E. 12 10

7. 7 12 8 11 9 10 10 ....   7.____
    A. 11 9   B. 9 8   C. 9 11   D. 10 11   E. 9 10

8. 13 13 12 15 15 14 17 ....   8.____
    A. 17 16   B. 14 17   C. 16 19   D. 19 19   E. 16 16

9. 19 18 12 17 16 13 15 ....   9.____
    A. 16 12   B. 14 14   C. 12 14   D. 14 12   E. 12 16

10. 7 15 12 8 16 13 9 ....   10.____
    A. 17 14   B. 17 10   C. 14 10   D. 14 17   E. 10 14

KEY (CORRECT ANSWERS)

1.	D	6.	B
2.	A	7.	C
3.	E	8.	A
4.	C	9.	B
5.	C	10.	A

TEST 7

DIRECTIONS : In each of the questions in this test, there is at the top a series of numbers which follow some definite order and, below, five sets of two numbers each. You are to look at the numbers in the series at the top and find out what order they follow. Then decide what the next two numbers in that series would be if the same order were continued. Next find these two numbers in one of the sets below. *PRINT THE LETTER OF THE CORRECT ANSWER IN THE SPACE AT THE RIGHT.*

1. 18 15 6 16 14 6 14 ....
   A. 12 6   B. 14 13   C. 6 12   D. 13 12   E. 13 6   1.____

2. 6 6 5 8 8 7 10 10 ....
   A. 8 12   B. 9 12   C. 12 12   D. 12 9   E. 9 9   2.____

3. 17 20 23 26 29 32 35 ....
   A. 37 40   B. 41 44   C. 38 41   D. 38 42   E. 36 39   3.____

4. 15 5 7 16 9 11 17 ....
   A. 18 13   B. 15 17   C. 12 19   D. 13 15   E. 12 13   4.____

5. 19 17 16 16 13 15 10 ....
   A. 14 7   B. 12 9   C. 14 9   D. 7 12   E. 10 14   5.____

6. 11 1 16 10 6 21 9 ....
   A. 12 26   B. 26 8   C. 11 26   D. 11 8   E. 8 11   6.____

7. 21 21 19 17 17 15 13 ....
   A. 11 11   B. 13 11   C. 11 9   D. 9 7   E. 13 13   7.____

8. 23 22 20 19 16 15 11 ....
   A. 6 5   B. 10 9   C. 6 1   D. 10 6   E. 10 5   8.____

9. 17 10 16 9 14 8 11 ....
   A. 7 11   B. 7 7   C. 10 4   D. 4 10   E. 7 4   9.____

10. 11 9 14 12 17 15 20 18 23 ....
    A. 21 24   B. 26 21   C. 21 26   D. 24 27   E. 26 29   10.____

KEY (CORRECT ANSWERS)

1. E	6. C
2. B	7. B
3. C	8. E
4. D	9. B
5. A	10. C

TEST 8

DIRECTIONS : In each of the questions in this test, there is at the top a series of numbers which follow some definite order and, below, five sets of two numbers each. You are to look at the numbers in the series at the top and find out what order they follow. Then decide what the next two numbers in that series would be if the same order were continued. Next find these two numbers in one of the sets below. *PRINT THE LETTER OF THE CORRECT ANSWER IN THE SPACE AT THE RIGHT.*

1. 13 4 5 13 6 7 13 ....   1.____

    A. 13 8   B. 8 13   C. 8 9   D. 8 8   E. 7 8

2. 10 10 9 11 11 10 12 ....   2.____

    A. 13 14   B. 12 11   C. 13 13   D. 12 12   E. 12 13

3. 6 6 8 10 10 12 14 ....   3.____

    A. 14 14   B. 14 16   C. 16 16   D. 12 14   E. 10 10

4. 8 1 9 3 10 5 11 ....   4.____

    A. 7 12   B. 6 12   C. 12 6   D. 7 8   E. 6 7

5. 30 11 24 12 19 14 15 17 12 21 10 ....   5.____

    A. 23 8   B. 25 8   C. 26 9   D. 24 9   E. 25 9

6. 24 30 29 22 28 27 19 26 25 15 24 ....   6.____

    A. 14 23   B. 19 18   C. 23 22   D. 25 11   E. 23 10

7. 7 5 9 7 11 9 13 ....   7.____

    A. 11 14   B. 10 15   C. 11 15   D. 12 14   E. 10 14

8. 9 10 11 7 8 9 5 ....   8.____

    A. 6 7   B. 7 8   C. 5 6   D. 6 4   E. 7 5

9. 8 9 10 10 9 10 11 11 10 11 12 ....   9.____

    A. 11 12   B. 12 10   C. 11 11   D. 12 11   E. 11 13

10. 5 6 8 9 12 13 17 18 23 24 ....   10.____

    A. 30 31   B. 25 31   C. 29 30   D. 25 30   E. 30 37

KEY (CORRECT ANSWERS)

1.	C		6.	E
2.	B		7.	C
3.	B		8.	A
4.	A		9.	D
5.	C		10.	A

12

TEST 9

DIRECTIONS : In each of the questions in this test, there is at the top a series of numbers which follow some definite order and, below, five sets of two numbers each. You are to look at the numbers in the series at the top and find out what order they follow. Then decide what the next two numbers in that series would be if the same order were continued. Next find these two numbers in one of the sets below. *PRINT THE LETTER OF THE CORRECT ANSWER IN THE SPACE AT THE RIGHT.*

1. 8 9 10 8 9 10 8 ....
    A. 89   B. 910   C. 98   D. 108   E. 810   1._____

2. 3 4 4 3 5 5 3....
    A. 33   B. 63   C. 36   D. 66   E. 6 7   2._____

3. 7 7 3 7 7 4 7....
    A. 77   B. 78   C. 57   D. 87   E. 75   3._____

4. 18 18 19 20 20 21 22 ....
    A. 22 23   B. 23 24   C. 23 23   D. 22 22   E. 21 22   4._____

5. 2 6 10 3 7 11 4 ....
    A. 12 16   B. 5 9   C. 8 5   D. 12 5   E. 8 12   5._____

6. 11 8 15 12 19 16 23 ....
    A. 27 20   B. 24 20   C. 27 24   D. 20 24   E. 20 27   6._____

7. 16 8 15 9 14 10 13 ....
    A. 12 11   B. 13 12   C. 11 13   D. 11 12   E. 11 14   7._____

8. 4 5 13 6 7 12 8 .0...
    A. 9 11   B. 13 9   C. 9 13   D. 11 9   E. 11 10   8._____

9. 3 8 4 9 5 10 6 11 7....
    A. 7 11   B. 7 8   C. 11 8   D. 12 7   E. 12 8   9._____

10. 18 14 19 17 20 20 21 ....
    A. 22 24   B. 14 19   C. 24 21   D. 21 23   E. 23 22   10._____

KEY (CORRECT ANSWERS)

1.	B		6.	E
2.	D		7.	D
3.	E		8.	A
4.	A		1.	E
5.	E		2.	E

ARITHMETIC
EXAMINATION SECTION
TEST 1

DIRECTIONS: Each question or ncomplete statement is followed by several suggested answers or completions. Select the one that BEST answers the question or completes the statement. *PRINT THE LETTER OF THE CORRECT ANSWER IN THE SPACE AT THE RIGHT.*

1. The result of a computation using only the numbers 8 and 7 is 15. In this computation, the number 15 is the

    A. product   B. sum   C. quotient
    D. difference   E. average

1._____

2. Which statement describes how to find the average of a group of scores?

    A. Find the sum of the scores and divide by 2.
    B. Find the sum of the scores and divide by the number of scores.
    C. Arrange the scores from lowest to highest and select the middle one.
    D. Take half the difference between the highest score and the lowest score.
    E. None of the above

2._____

3.
```
  6428
   974
    86
  7280
   763
  5407
```

    A. 19,838   B. 20,828   C. 20,838   D. 20,928   E. 20,938

3._____

4. What is the inverse operation used to check division?

    A. Addition   B. Subtraction   C. Multiplication
    D. Division   E. None of the above

4._____

5. What is the ratio of 1 inch to 1 yard?
1 to _____.

    A. 1   B. 3   C. 12   D. 24   E. 36

5._____

6. Which of the following is NOT evenly divisible by 8?

    A. 6   B. 8   C. 40   D. 72   E. 104

6._____

7. Each of the numerals listec below represents a number of feet. Which numeral MOST NEARLY represents the height of an average American man?

    A. .059   B. 0.59   C. 5.90   D. 59.0   E. 590

7._____

Questions 8-9.

DIRECTIONS: Question 8 and 9 are to be answered on the basis of the following line.

8.   The point halfway between W and X would correspond to   8._____

   A.   4   B.   4 1/2   C.   5   D.   5 1/2   E.   6

9.   What number would correspond to point P if it is placed on the number line so that P is   9._____
     between X and Y, and W is between P and X?

   A.   6   B.   7 1/2
   C.   9   D.   10
   E.   No such point can exist

10.   What is the GREATEST common divisor of 24, 40, and 120?   10._____

   A.   2   B.   4   C.   8   D.   10   E.   12

11.   Which of these is NOT equal to 4/9?   11._____

   A.   2/3   B.   20/45   C.   8/18   D.   16/36   E.   12/27

12.   For which pair of the following operations are the rules for placing the decimal point in the   12._____
      answer the SAME?
            I.   Addition
            II. Subtraction
            III. Multiplication
            IV. Division
      The CORRECT answer is:

   A.   I and II   B.   I and III   C.   II and IV   D.   III and IV
   E.   The rules are different for each operation

13.   Three of four identical measuring containers are filled   13._____
      as shown at the right. All the liquid in the three con-
      tainers is poured into the empty container on the right.
      What fractional part of this container will be filled?

        $\frac{3}{10}$ $\frac{1}{5}$ $\frac{8}{20}$

   A.   1/10   B.   12/35   C.   7/10   D.   9/10   E.   1

14.   1/2 of 20 is the same as 1/4 of   14._____

   A.   5   B.   10   C.   40   D.   60   E.   80

15. What is the SMALLEST number which can be divided evenly by each of the following numbers: 4, 6, 8?   15.____

    A. 48   B. 32   C. 24   D. 16   E. 12

16.____

16. $(2/3 \div 1/2) \times \dfrac{1}{2} =$

    A. 1/6   B. 3/8   C. 2/3   D. 3/2   E. 8/3

17. A bank clerk reported that the number of $100 bills in the vault was 10,003. About how much money is this?   17.____

    A. $1,000   B. $10,000   C. $100,000
    D. $1,000,000   E. $10,000,000

18. 3/40 is the same as   ¯8.____

    A. .0075   B. .0133   C. .075   D. .1333   E. .75

19.____

19. $\begin{array}{r} 9\,4/5 \\ +13\,1/4 \\ \hline \end{array}$

    A. 22 5/9   B. 22 9/20   C. 23   D. 23 1/20   E. 23 1/5

20. $\begin{array}{r} 36 \\ 52\overline{)1872} \end{array}$ 20.____

To make the answer in the example above four times as large as it is, you could change the number 1872 to

    A. 208   B. 468   C. 936   D. 3944   E. 7488

21. Which of these will produce an even whole number no matter what whole number is put in place of A?   21.____

    I. $2 \times \triangle + 1$
    II. $2 \times \triangle + 2$
    III. $2 \times \triangle + 3$

The CORRECT answer is:

    A. I *only*   B. II *only*   C. III *only*
    D. I and II *only*   E. I and III *only*

22. Which of these shows the CORRECT meaning of 407?   22.____

    A. (4 x ten) + (7 x one)
    B. (4 x ten x ten) + (0 x ten) + (7 x one)
    C. (4 + 0 + 7) x (one hundred)
    D. (4 x one) + (0 x ten) + (7 x ten x ten)
    E. (4 x one) + (7 x ten)

23. If the scale length of 4 1/2 inches represents an actual distance of 72 miles, how many miles does the scale length of 7 inches represent?   23.____

    A. 2   B. 56   C. 74 1/2   D. 112   E. 504

24.
```
4  5  6  .  7  2  3  8
↑  ↑        ↑  ↑  ↑
F  G        H  J  K
```
In the above numeral, which arrow points to the hundreds place?

   A. F   B. G   C. H   D. J   E. K

24._____

25. Which of these is between 5/6 and 7/8?

   A. 2/3   B. 3/4   C. 4/5   D. 6/7   E. 8/9

25._____

26. $340.292 \div 48.2 =$

   A. 706   B. 76   C. 70.6   D. 7.6   E. 7.06

26._____

27. Jim started mowing the grass at 1:45 P.M. and finished at 2:15 P.M.
How many minutes did Jim take to mow the grass?

   A. 30   B. 70   C. 90   D. 180   E. 240

27._____

28. To reduce a fraction to LOWEST terms, what should be done to both numerator and denominator?

   A. Each should be divided by 2.
   B. Each should be multiplied by 2.
   C. Each should be multiplied by the least common multiple.
   D. Each should be divided by the greatest common divisor.
   E. The same number should be subtracted from each.

28._____

29. $3+\sqrt{64} =$

   A. 11   B. 19   C. 24   D. 35   E. $\sqrt{73}$

29._____

30. Between 8 A.M. and 3 P.M., the temperature rose 25°. The temperature at 8 A.M. was 10° below zero.
At 3 P.M., the temperature was _____ zero.

   A. 25° above   B. 15° above   C. 5 °above
   D. 5° below   E. 35° below

30._____

31. A boy saves 18 dollars in 8 weeks. He continues to save at the same rate.
How many weeks will it take him to save 81 dollars?

   A. 13   B. 36   C. 40   D. 71   E. 182 1/4

31._____

32. One whole number is divided by another whole number.
It is ALWAYS TRUE that the

   A. divisor is smaller than the quotient
   B. remainder is smaller than the divisor
   C. quotient is smaller than the divisor
   D. remainder is smaller than the quotient
   E. dividend is smaller than the remainder

32._____

33. Which of these will NEVER change the value of a number?
    I.   Multiplying it by 1
    II. Dividing it by 1
    III. Multiplying it by its reciprocal
    The CORRECT answer is:

    A. I only   B. II only   C. III only
    D. I and II only   E. I and III only

33.____

34. Which of the following equals 7 x (3 + 9)?

    A. (7 x 3) + (7 x 9)   B. (7 x 9) + (3 x 9)
    C. (7 x 3) +(3x9)   D. 7 x 27
    E. 21 + 9

34.____

35.

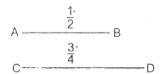

    in the above figure $\dfrac{\text{length of AB}}{\text{length of CD}} =$

    A. 1/2   B. 1/3   C. 2/3   D. 3/2   E. 5/3

35.____

36. Which series is NOT in descending order?

    A. 4.04, 4.004, .404   B. 2.1, 1.2, 1.12
    C. .06, .009, .10   D. 13.2, 12.3, 12.03
    E. 736, 631, 367

36.____

Questions 37-38.

DIRECTIONS: Questions 37 and 38 are to be answered on the basis of the following graph.

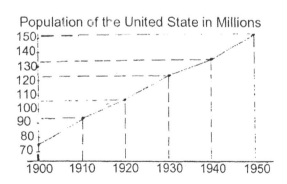

Population of the United State in Millions

37. According to the above graph, the population of the United States in 1935 was about

    A. 127,000   B. 1,270,000
    C. 12,700,000   D. 127,000,000
    E. 1,270,000,000

37.____

38. What was the AVERAGE increase per year between 1900 and 1950?   38.____

    A. 1,500   B. 15,000   C. 150,000
    D. 750,000   E. 1,500,000

39. What is the ratio of 2 gallons to 3 quarts?   39.____

    A. 8 to 3   B. 3 to 8   C. 3 to 2   D. 2 to 3   E. 1 to 6

40. What percent of the figure at the right is darkened?   40.____
    A. 12
    B. 25
    C. 48
    D. 50
    E. 52

41. A cutting edge .004 inch thick is four times as thick as a second cutting edge.   41.____
    How many inches thick is the second cutting edge?

    A. .001   B. .0032   C. .004   D. .016   E. .04

42.____

42. 20% is equal to the fraction $\dfrac{?}{30}$.

    A. 2/3   B. 6   C. 60   D. 150   E. 600

43. In the figure at the right, the two bars whose lengths have the ratio 2 to 1 are   43.____
    A. II and III
    B. IV and I
    C. IV and III
    D. I and III
    E. IV and II

44. The advertisement for a sale reads: *All books reduced more than 20%.*   44.____
    If two books each have the same sale price, which statement MUST be TRUE?
    The

    A. original prices of both books were the same
    B. original prices of both books were different
    C. percent reduction for both books was the same
    D. sale price of each book is less than 80% of the original price
    E. sale price of each book is more than 80% of the original price

45. Which of these multiplications will result in an odd number?   45.____

    I.
$$
\begin{array}{r}
3\ 0\ 4\ 9 \\
\times\ 6\ 4\ 3\ 1 \\
\hline
\end{array}
$$

    II.
$$
\begin{array}{r}
7\ 0\ 0\ 2 \\
\times\ 3\ 4\ 8\ 5 \\
\hline
\end{array}
$$

    III.
$$
\begin{array}{r}
6\ 5\ 4\ 3 \\
\times\ 3\ 4\ 5\ 6 \\
\hline
\end{array}
$$

    IV.
$$
\begin{array}{r}
8\ 7\ 6\ 5 \\
\times\ 3\ 4\ 9\ 7 \\
\hline
\end{array}
$$

The CORRECT answer is:

A. I and III *only*   B. I and IV *only*
C. II and IV *only*   D. II, III, and IV *only*
E. All of the above

46. A movie opened in a theatre on April 6 and was shown every day through April 27.   46.____
On how many days was it shown?

A. 20   B. 21   C. 22
D. 23   E. None of the above

47. A student has an average of 80 for three tests.   47.____
What must he score on the next test in order to obtain an average of 84?

A. 80   B. 84   C. 88   D. 92   E. 96

48. Of 28 students in a class, 25 contributed to the Junior Red Cross and 16 to the March of   48.____
Dimes. Every member of the class contributed to AT LEAST one of the two organizations.
The number who contributed to both is

A. 3   B. 12   C. 13   D. 16   E. 25

49. On an arithmetic test, Bill got 32 as an answer to one problem. In working this problem,   49.____
Bill's *only* mistake was multiplying by 4 in the last step when he should have divided by 4.
What is the CORRECT answer to the problem?

A. 2
B. 4
C. 8
D. 28
E. It cannot be determined from the information given.

50. Each of two whole numbers is greater than 1. Their product is an odd number. Then, their sum is a(n) _____ their product.

50.____

   A. odd number less than
   B. even number less than
   C. odd number greater than
   D. even number greater than
   E. number equal to

———————

KEY (CORRECT ANSWERS)

1.	B	11.	A	21.	B	31.	B	41.	A
2.	B	12.	A	22.	B	32.	B	42.	B
3.	E	13.	D	23.	D	33.	D	43.	A
4.	C	14.	C	24.	A	34.	A	44.	D
5.	E	15.	C	25.	D	35.	C	45.	B
6.	A	16.	C	26.	E	36.	C	46.	C
7.	C	17.	D	27.	A	37.	D	47.	E
8.	C	18.	C	28.	D	38.	E	48.	C
9.	E	19.	D	29.	A	39.	A	49.	A
10.	C	20.	E	30.	B	40.	E	50.	B

———————

SOLUTIONS TO PROBLEMS

1. 8 and 7 yield 15 by using sum, since 8 + 7 = 15.

2. To average out a group of numbers, add them and divide by the number of numbers. Ex.: The average of 3, 4, 8 = (3 + 4 + 8)/3 = 5.

3. 6428 + 974 + 86 + 7280 + 763 + 5407 = 20,938

4. The inverse of division is multiplication. Ex.: To check that
    $10 \div 2 = 5$, we note that (5)(2) = 10.

5. 1 in. to 1 yd. = 1 in. to 36 in. = 1 to 36

6. 6 is not evenly divisible by 8 since whole number.

7. 5.90 ft. = 5 ft. 10.8 in., which is a reasonable man's height.

8. $(2 + 8) \div 2 = 5$

9. If P is between X and Y, it corresponds to a point between 8 and 12. It would be impossible for W to be between P and X.

10. The greatest common divisor of 24, 40, and 120 is 8 since $24 \div 8$, $40 \div 8$, and $120 \div 8$ all yield whole numbers. No number larger than 8 will divide evenly into each of 24, 40, and 120.

11. $\frac{2}{3} \neq \frac{4}{9}$ because $(2)(9) \neq (3)(4)$

12. For addition and subtraction, the rules for placing the decimal point in the answer are alike, namely, to line up the decimal point for each number.

13. $\frac{3}{10} + \frac{1}{5} + \frac{8}{20} = \frac{3}{10} + \frac{2}{10} + \frac{4}{10} = \frac{9}{10}$

14. Let x = missing number. Then, $(\frac{1}{2})(20) = \frac{1}{4}x$. $10 = \frac{1}{4}x$, so $x = 40$

15. 24 is the smallest number which can divide evenly by 4, 6, and 8. This is called the least common multiple.

16. $(\frac{2}{3} \div \frac{1}{2}) \times \frac{1}{2} = \frac{4}{3} \times \frac{1}{2} = \frac{4}{6} = \frac{2}{3}$

17. $(10{,}003)(\$100) = \$1{,}000{,}300 \approx \$1{,}000{,}000$

18. $\dfrac{3}{40} = .075$

19. $9\dfrac{4}{5} + 13\dfrac{1}{4} = 9\dfrac{16}{20} + 13\dfrac{5}{20} = 22\dfrac{21}{20} = 23\dfrac{1}{20}$

20. Using 7488, we get $7488 \div 52 = 144$, , which is 4 times as large as 36.

21. $2x + 2$ must be even if x = any whole number. The other choices $2x + 1$ and $2x + 3$ must be odd.

22. $407 = (4 \text{ x ten x ten}) + (0 \text{ x ten}) + (7 \text{ x one})$

23. Let x = actual miles. Then, $\dfrac{4\frac{1}{2}}{72} = \dfrac{7}{x}, \ 4\dfrac{1}{2}x = 504, x = 112$

24. F points to 4, which is in the hundreds place.

25. $\dfrac{6}{7}$ lies between $\dfrac{5}{6}$ and $\dfrac{7}{8}$. To check convert to decimals, $.85714\overline{2}$ is between $.8\overline{3}$ and $.875$.

26. $340.292 \div 48.2 = 7.06$

27. From 1:45 PM to 2:15 PM = 30 minutes

28. To completely reduce a fraction, each of numerator and denominator should be divided by the greatest common divisor.

    Ex.: $\dfrac{18}{30}$ can be reduced to by dividing numerator and denominator by 6. Note: 6 = greatest common divisor of 18 and 30.

29. $3 + \sqrt{64} = 3 + 8 = 11$

30. $-10^{o} + 25^{o} = 15^{o}$ above zero

31. $\$81 \div \$18 = 4.5$. Then, $(4.5)(8) = 36$ weeks

32. When dividing one whole number by another whole number, the remainder must be smaller than the divisor.
    Ex.: $39 \div 17 = 2$ with a remainder of 5, and $5 < 17$.

33. Dividing by 1 or multiplying by 1 will never change the value of a number.
    Ex.: $9 = (9)(1) = 9 \div 1$

34. $7 \times (3 + 9). = 84 = (7 \times 3) + (7 \times 9)$

35. $\dfrac{1}{2}" \div \dfrac{3}{4}" = (\dfrac{1}{2})(\dfrac{4}{3}) = \dfrac{4}{6} = \dfrac{2}{3}$

36. .06, .009, .10 is NOT in descending order. The correct order would be .10, .06, .009.

37. In 1935, the population of the U.S. was about 127,000,000.

38. Average increase $= (150,000,000 - 75,000,000) \div 50 = 1,500,000$

39. 2 gallons = 8 quarts, so 2 gallons : 3 quarts = 8:3

40. There are 13 darkened boxes out of a total of 25 boxes.
    $\dfrac{13}{25} = 52\%.$

41. Second cutting edge $= .004" \div 4 = .001$ in.

42. $20\% = \dfrac{1}{5} = \dfrac{6}{30}$

43. Bar II = 3 units, bar III = 1 1/2 units, and 3 to 1 1/2 = 2 to 1.

44. If a price is reduced by more than 20%, the sales price MUST be less than 80% of the original price. Ex: Original price = $100, reduced by 22%, sales price = $78 = 78% of original price.

45. Since 9x1= odd and 5x7= odd, both (3049)(6431) and (8765)(3497) must result in an odd number.

46. $27 - 6 + 1 = 22$ days

47. Let x = score on 4th test. Then, $(80)(3) + x = (84)(4)$. $240 \div x = 336$. . Solving, x = 96

48. Let x = number who contributed to both, 25 - x = number who contributed only to Junior Red Cross, 16 - x = number who contributed only to March of Dimes. Then, x+25-x+16-x =28, so x = 13.

49. Since he multiplied by 4, the next to last number = 8. So, $8 \div 4 = 2$.

50. Since their product is odd, each number must be odd. Their sum is an even number less than their product.
    Ex: $3 + 5 = 8 < (3)(5) = 15$

BASIC FUNDAMENTALS OF BOOKKEEPING

CONTENTS

BASIC FUNDAMENTALS OF BOOKKEEPING

I. INTRODUCTION

Why keep records? If you are a typical small-business man, your answer to this question is probably, "Because the Government requires it!" And if the question comes in the middle of a busy day, you may add a few heartfelt words about the amount of time you have to spend on records--just for the Government.

Is it "just for the Government," though? True, regulations of various governmental agencies have greatly increased the record-keeping requirements of business. But this may be a good thing for the small-business man overburdened though he is.

Many small-business managers don't recognize their bookkeeping records for what they can really do. Their attitudes concerning these records are typified by one businessman who said, "Records only tell you what you have done in the past. It's too late to do anything about the past; I need to know what is going to happen in the future. "However, the past can tell us much about what may happen in the future; and, certainly we can profit in the future from knowledge of our past mistakes.

These same managers may recognize that records are necessary in filing their tax returns, or that a banker requires financial information before he will lend money, but often their appreciation of their bookkeeping systems ends at this point. However, there are many ways in which the use of such information can help an owner manage his business more easily and profitably.

The small-businessman is confronted with an endless array of problems and decisions every day. Sound decisions require an informed manager; and many management problems can be solved with the aid of the right bookkeeping information.

II. REQUIREMENTS OF A GOOD RECORD SYSTEM

Of course, to get information that is really valuable to you--to get the right information-- requires a good bookkeeping system. What are the characteristics of a good system? You want one that is simple and easy to understand, reliable, accurate, consistent, and one that will get the information to you promptly.

A simple, well-organized system of records, regularly kept up, can actually be a timesaver--by bringing order out of disorder. Furthermore, competition is very strong in today's business areas. A businessman needs to know almost on a day-to-day basis where his business stands profit wise, which lines of merchandise or services are the most or the least profitable, what his working-capital needs are, and many other details. He can get this information with reasonable certainty only if he has a good recordkeeping system—one that gives him all the information he needs.

In setting up a recordkeeping system that is tailored to your business, you will probably need the professional help of a competent accountant. And you may want to retain the services of an accountant or bookkeeper to maintain these records. But it is your job to learn to interpret this information and to use it effectively.

One of the reasons that many managers have misgivings about keeping records is that they don't understand them or know how they can be used. The owner or manager of a small business may be an expert in his line of business; however, he generally does not have a background in keeping records. So he is usually confused. What we will try to do in this discussion is to highlight the "why and what of bookkeeping." In so-doing, we aim to eliminate that confusion.

III. IMPORTANT BOOKKEEPING RECORDS

Today's managers should be familiar with the following bookkeeping records:

- Journal
- Ledgers
- Balance sheet
- Income statement
- Funds flow statement

We will discuss each of them in turn. In addition, a brief discussion of other supporting records will be made.

A. Bookkeeping Books

The journal, which accountants call "the book of original entry," is a chronological record of all business transactions engaged in by the firm. It is simply a financial diary. The ledgers, or "books of account," are more specialized records used to classify the journal entries according to like elements. For example, there would be a separate ledger account for cash entries, another for all sales, and still others for items such as accounts receivable, inventory, and loans. All transactions are first entered in the journal, and then posted in the appropriate ledger. The journal and ledgers are of minor importance to the manager in making decisions, but they play a vital role for the accountant or bookkeeper because the more important accounting statements such as the balance sheet and the income statement are derived from the journal and ledger entries.

B. Financial Reports

The two principal financial reports in most businesses are the balance sheet and the income statement. Up to about 25 or 30 years ago, the balance sheet was generally considered to be the most important financial statement. Until that time, it was generally used only as a basis for the extension of credit and bank loans, and very little thought was given to the information it offered that might be important in „the operation and management of the business. Starting about 30 years ago, emphasis has gradually shifted to the income statement. Today the balance sheet and income statements are of equal importance, both to the accountant in financial reporting and to the manager faced with a multitude of administrative problems.

Essentially, the balance sheet shows what a business has, what it owes, and the investment of the owners in the business. It can be likened to a snapshot, showing the financial condition of the business *at a certain point in time.* The income statement, on the other hand, is a summary of business operations for a certain period--usually between two balance sheet dates. The income statement can be compared to a moving picture; it indicates the activity of a business *over a certain period of time.* In very general terms, the balance sheet tells you where you are, and the income statement tells you how you got there since the last time you had a balance sheet prepared.

Both the balance sheet and income statement can be long and complicated documents. Both accountants and management need some device that can highlight the critical financial information contained in these complex documents. Certain standard ratios or relationships between items on the financial statements have been developed that allow the interested parties to quickly determine important characteristics of the firm's activities. There are many relationships that might be important in a specific business that would not be as significant in another.

Other devices of the bookkeeper, such as funds flow statements, daily summaries of sales and cash receipts, the checkbook, account receivable records, property depreciation records, and insurance scheduling have also been found useful to management.

C. The Balance Sheet

As stated earlier, the balance sheet represents what a business has, what it owes, and the investment of the owners. The things of value that the business has or owns are called *assets*. The claims of creditors against these assets are called liabilities. The value of the assets over and above the *liabilities* can be justifiably called the owner's claim. This amount is usually called the owner's equity (or net worth).

This brings us to the *dual-aspect concept* of bookkeeping. The balance sheet is set up to portray two aspects of each entry or event recorded on it. For each thing of value, or asset, there is a claim against that asset. The recognition of this concept leads to the balance sheet formula: ASSETS = LIABILITIES + OWNER'S EQUITY. Let's take an example to clarify this concept. Suppose Joe Smith decides to start a business. He has $2,000 cash in the bank. He got this sum by investing $1,000 of his own money and by borrowing $1,000 from the bank. If he were to draw up a balance sheet at this time, he would have assets of $2 000 cash balanced against a liability claim of $1,000 and an owner's claim of $1,000. Using the balance sheet formula: $2,000 = $1,000 + $1,000. This formula means there will always be a balance between assets and claims against them. The balance sheet *always* balances unless there has been a clerical error.

The balance sheet is usually, constructed in a two-column format. The assets appear in the left hand column and the claims against the assets (the liabilities and owner's equity) are in the right hand column. Other formats are sometimes used; but, in any case, the balance sheet is-an itemized or detailed account of the basic formula: as sets = liabilities + owner's equity.

1. Assets

I have been speaking of assets belonging to the business. Of course, the business does not legally own anything unless it is organized as a corporation. But regardless of whether the business is organized as a proprietorship, a partnership, or a corporation, all business book-keeping should be reckoned and accounted apart from the accounting of the personal funds and assets of, its owners.

Assets are typically classified into three categories:

- Current assets
- Fixed assets
- Other assets

a. Current Assets

For bookkeeping purposes, the term "current assets" is used to designate cash and other assets which can be converted to cash during the normal operating cycle of the business (usually one year). The distinction between current assets and noncurrent assets is important since lenders and others pay much attention to the total amount of current assets. The size of current assets has a significant relationship to the stability of the business because it represents, to some degree, the amount of cash that might be raised quickly to meet current obligations. Here are some of the major current asset items.

Cash consists of funds that are immediately available to use without restrictions. These funds are usually in the form of checking-account deposits in banks, cash-register money, and petty cash. Cash should be large enough to meet obligations that are immediately due.

Accounts, receivable are Arricnint8 'Owed to the company by its customers as a result of sales. Essentially, these accounts are the result of granting credit to customers. They may take the form of charge accounts where no interest or service charge is made, or they may be of an interest-bearing nature. In either case they are a drain on working capital. The more that is outstanding on accounts receivable, the less money that is available to meet current needs. The trick with accounts receivable is to keep them small enough so as not to endanger working capital, but large enough to keep from losing sales to credit-minded customers.

Inventory is defined as those items which are held for sale in the ordinary course of business, or which are to be consumed in the production of goods and services that are to be sold. Since accountants are conservative by nature, they include in inventory only items that are salable, and these items are valued at cost or market value, whichever is lower? Control of inventory and inventory expenses is one of management's most important jobs-particularly for retailers--and good bookkeeping records in this area are particularly useful.

Prepaid expenses represent assets, paid for in advance, but whose usefulness will usually expire in a short time. A good example of this is prepaid insurance. A business pays for insurance protection in advance--usually three to five years in advance. The right to this protection is a thing of value--an asset--and the unused portion can be refunded or converted to cash.

b. Fixed Assets

"Fixed assets" are items owned by the business that have relatively long life. These assets are used in the production or sale of other goods and services. If they were held for resale, they would be classified as inventory, even though they might be long-lived assets.

Normally these assets are composed of land, buildings, and equipment. Some companies lump their fixed assets into one entry on their balance sheets, but you gain more information and can exercise more control over these assets if they are listed separately on the balance sheet. You may even want to list various types of equipment separately.

There is one other aspect of fixed-asset bookkeeping that we should discuss--and this is depreciation. Generally fixed assets-with the exception of land-depreciate, or decrease in value with the passing of time. That is, a building or piece of equipment that is five years old is not worth as much as it was when it was new. For a balance sheet to show the true value of these assets, it must reflect this loss in value. For both tax and other accounting purposes, the businessman is allowed to deduct this loss in value each year over the useful life of the assets, until, over a period of time, he has deducted the total cost of the asset. There are several accepted ways to calculate how much of an asset's value can be deducted for depreciation in a given year. Depreciation is allowed as an expense item on the income statement, and we will discuss this fact later.

c. Other Assets

"Other assets" is a miscellaneous category. It accounts for any investments of the firm in securities, such as stock in other private companies or government bonds. It also includes intangible assets such as goodwill, patents, and franchise costs. Items in the "other-assets" category have a longer life than current-asset items.

2. Liabilities

"Liabilities" are the amounts of money owed by the business to people other than the owners. They are claims against the company's total assets, although they are not claims against any specific asset, except in the cases of some mortgages and equipment liens. Essentially, liabilities are divided into two classes:

Current liabilities

Long-term Liabilities

a. Current Liabilities

The term "current liabilities" is used to describe those claims of outsiders on the business that will fall, due within one year. Here are some of the more important current-liabilities entries on the balance sheet:

Accounts payable represent the amounts owed to vendors, wholesalers, and other suppliers from whom the business has bought items on account. This includes any items of inventory, supply, or capital equipment which have been purchased on credit and for which payment is expected in less than one year. For example, a retail butcher purchased 500 pounds of meat for $250, a quantity of fish that cost $50, and a new air-conditioning unit for his store for $450. He bought all of these items on 60-day terms. His accounts payable were increased by $750. Of course, at the same time his inventory increased by $300 and his fixed assets rose by $450. If he had paid cash for these items, his accounts payable would not have been affected, but his cash account would have decreased by $750, thus keeping the accounting equation in balance.

Short-term loans, which are sometimes called notes payable, are loans from individuals, banks, or other lending institutions which fall due within a year. Also included in this category is the portion of any long-term debt that will come due within a year.

Accrued expenses are obligations which the company has incurred, but for which there has been no formal bill or invoice as yet. An example of this is accrued taxes. The owner knows the business has the obligation to pay taxes; and they are accruing or accumulating each day. The fact that the taxes do not have to be paid until a later date does not diminish the obligation. Another example of accrued expenses is wages. Although wages are paid weekly or monthly, they are being earned hourly or daily and constitute a valid claim against the company. An accurate balance sheet will reflect these obligations.

b. Long-Term Liabilities

Claims of outsiders on the business that do not come due within one year are called "long-term liabilities" or, simply, "other liabilities." Included in this category are bonded indebtedness, mortgages, and long-term loans from individuals, banks, and others from whom the business may borrow money, such as the SBA. As was stated before, any part of a long-term debt that falls due within one year from the date of the balance sheet would be recorded as part of the current liabilities of the business.

Owner's Equity

The owner's equity section of the balance sheet is located on the right-hand side underneath the listing of the liabilities. It shows the claims of the owners on the company. Essentially, this is a balancing figure--that is, the owners get what's left of the assets after the liability claims have been recognized. This is an obvious definition, if you will remember the balance sheet formula. Transposing the formula as we learned it a few minutes ago, it becomes Assets - Liabilities = Owner's Equity. In the case where the business is a sole proprietorship, it is customary to show owner's equity as one entry with no distinction being made between the owner's initial investment and the accumulated retained earnings of the business. However, in the case of an incorporated business, there are entries for stockholders' claims as well as for earnings that have been accumulated and retained in the business. Of course, if the business has been consistently operating at a loss, the proprietor's claim may be less than his initial investment. And, in the case of a corporation, the balancing account could be operating deficit rather than retained earnings.

If we put together the entries we have been talking about, we have a complete balance sheet. There is a lot of information in this statement. It tells you just what you have and where it is. It also tells you what you owe. You need this information to help you decide what actions you should take in running your business. If you need to borrow money, the banker or anyone else from whom you borrow will want to look at your balance sheet.

D. THE INCOME STATEMENT

In recent years the income statement has become as important as the balance sheet as a financial and management record. It is also called the profit and loss statement, or simply the P and L statement. This financial record summarizes the activities of the company over a period of time, listing those that can be expressed in dollars. That is, it reports the revenues of the company and the expenses incurred in. obtaining the revenues, and it shows the profit or loss resulting from these activities. The income statement complements the balance sheet. While balance sheet analysis shows the change in position of the company at the end of accounting periods, the income statement shows how the change took place during the accounting period. Both reports 'are necessary for a full understanding of the operation of the business.

The income statement for particular company should be tailored to fit the activities of that company, and there is no rigid format that must be followed in constructing this report. But the following categories are found in most income statements.

1. Sales

The major activity of most businesses is the sales of products and services, and the bulk of revenue comes from sales. In recording sales, the figure used is net sales-that is, sales after discounts, allowances, and returned goods have been accounted for.

2. Cost of Goods Sold

Another important item, in calculating profit or loss, is the cost of the goods that the company has sold. This item is difficult to calculate accurately. Since the goods sold come from inventory, and since the company may have bought parts of its inventory at several prices, it is hard to determine exactly what is the cost of the particular part of the inventory that was sold. In large companies, and particularly in companies using cost accounting, there are some rather complicated methods of determining "cost of goods sold, " but they are beyond the scope of this presentation. However, there is a simple, generally accepted way of calculating cost of goods sold. In this method you simply add the net amount of purchases during the accounting period to your beginning inventory, and subtract from this your ending inventory. The result can be considered cost-of-goods sold.

3. Gross Margin

The difference between sales and cost of goods sold is called the "gross margin" or gross profit. This item is often expressed as a percentage of sales, as well as in dollar figures. The percentage gross margin is a very significant figure because it indicates what the average markup is on the merchandise sold. So, if a manager knows his expenses as a percentage of sales, he can calculate the mark up necessary to obtain the gross margin he needs for a profitable operation. It is surprising how many small-business men do not know what basis to use in setting markups. In fact, with the various, allowances, discounts, and markdowns that a business may offer, many managers do not know what their markup actually is. The gross margin calculation on the income statement can help the manager with this problem.

There are other costs of running a business besides the cost of the goods sold. When you use the simple method of determining costs of goods sold, these costs are called "expenses."

For example, here are some typical expenses: salaries and wages, utilities, depreciation, interest, administrative expenses, supplies, bad debts, advertising, and taxes--Federal, State, and local. These are typical expenses, but there are many other kinds of expenses that may be experienced by other businesses. For example, we have shown in the Blank Company's balance sheet that he owns his own land and building--with a mortgage, of course. These accounts for part of his depreciation and interest expenses, but for a company that rents its quarters, rent would appear as the expense item. Other common expenses are traveling expense, commissions, and advertising.

Most of these expense items are self-explanatory, but there are a few that merit further comment. For one thing, the salary or draw of the owner should be recorded among the expenses--either as a part of salaries and wages or as part of administrative expenses. To exclude the owner's compensation from expenses distorts the actual profitability of the business. And, if the company is incorporated, it would reduce the allowable tax deductions of the business. Of course, for tax purposes, the owner's salary or draw in a proprietorship or partnership is considered as part of the net profit.

We discussed depreciation when we examined the balance sheet, and we mentioned that it was an item of expense. Although no money is actually paid out for depreciation, it is a real expense because it represents reduction in the value of the assets.

The most important thing about expenses is to be sure to include all of the expenses that the business incurs. This not only helps the owner get a more accurate picture of his operation but it allows him to take full advantage of the tax deductions that legitimate expenses offer.

4. Net Profit

In a typical company when expenses are subtracted from gross margin, the remainder is profit. However, if the business receives revenue from sources other than sales, such as rents, dividends on securities held by the company, or interest on money loaned by the company, it is added to profit at this point. For bookkeeping purposes, the resulting profit is labeled "profit before taxes:" This is the figure from which Federal income taxes are figured. If the business is a proprietorship, the profit is taxed as part of the owner's income. If the business is a corporation, the profits may be taxed on the basis of the corporate income tax schedule. When income taxes have been accounted for, the resultant entry is called "net profit after taxes," or simply "net profit." This is usually the final entry on the income statement.

Another financial record which managers can use to advantage is the funds flow statement. This statement is also called statement of sources and uses of funds and sometimes the "where got--where gone" statement. Whatever you call it, a record of sources and uses of past funds is useful to the manager. He can use it to evaluate past performance, and as a guide in determining future uses and sources of money.

When we speak of "funds" we do not necessarily mean actual "dollars" or "cash." Although accounting records are all written in monetary terms, they do not always involve an exchange of money. Many times in business transactions, it is credit rather than dollars that changes hands. Therefore, when we speak of funds flow, we are speaking of exchanges of *economic values* rather than merely the physical flow of dollars.

Basically, funds are used to: increase assets and reduce liabilities. They are also sometimes used to reduce owner's equity. An example of this would be the use of company funds to buy up outstanding stock or to buy out a partner. Where do funds come from? The three basic sources of funds are a reduction in assets, increases in liabilities, and increased owner's equity. All balance sheet items can be affected by the obtaining and spending of company fund's.

To examine the construction and use of a funds flow statement, let's take another look at the Blank Company. Here we show comparative balance sheets for two one-year periods. For the sake of simplicity, we have included only selected items from the balance sheets for analysis. Notice that the company gained funds by:

reducing cash $300,

increasing accounts payable $400,

putting $500 more owner's equity in the business, and

plowing back $800 of the profit into the business.

These funds were used to:

increase accounts receivable $300,
increase inventory $200,

buy $500 worth of equipment, and

pay off $1, 000 worth of long-term debt.

This funds flow statement has indicated to Mr. Blank where he has gotten his funds and how he has spent them. He can analyze these figures in the light of his plans and objectives and take appropriate action.

For example, if Mr. Blank wants to answer the question "Should I buy new capital equipment?" a look at his funds flow statement would show him his previous sources of funds, and it would give him a clue as to whether he could obtain funds for any new equipment.

I V. OTHER RECORDS

Up to this point, we have been talk ng about the basic types of bookkeeping records. In addition, we have discussed the two basic financial statements of a business: the balance sheet and the profit and loss statement. Now let us give our attention briefly to some other records which are very helpful to running a business successfully.

One element that appears on the balance sheet which I believe we can agree is important is cash. Because it is the lifeblood of all business, cash should be controlled and safe-guarded at all times. The daily summary of sales and cash receipts and the checkbook are used by many manager s of small businesses to help provide that control.

A. Daily Summary of Sales and Cash. Receipts

Not all businesses summarize the r daily transactions. However, a daily summary of sales and cash receipts is a very useful tool for checking how your business is doing on a day-to-day basis. At the close of each day's business, the actual cash on hand is counted and "balanced" against the total of the receipts recorded for the day. This balancing is done by means of the Daily Summary of Sales and Cash Receipts. This is a recording of every cash 'receipt and every charge sale, whether you use a cash register or sales checks or both. If you have more than one cash register, a daily summary should be prepared for each; the individual cash-register summaries can then be combined into one overall summary for convenience in handling.

In the daily summary form used for purposes of illustration, (see Handout), the first section, "Cash Receipts," records the total of all cash taken in during the day from whatever source. This is the cash that must be accounted for over and above, the amount in the change and/ or petty cash funds. We shall touch upon these two funds later. The three components of cash receipts are (1) cash sales, (2) collections on accounts, and (3) miscellaneous receipts.

The daily total of cash sales is obtained from a cash-register tape reading or, if no cash register is used, by totaling the cash-sales checks.

For collections on accounts, an individual record of each customer payment on account should be kept, whether or not these collections are rung up on a cash register. The amount to be entered on the daily summary is obtained by totaling these individual records.

Miscellaneous receipts are daily cash transactions that cannot be classified as sales or collections. They might include refunds from suppliers for overpayment, advertising rebates or allowances, . collections of rent from sub-leases or concessions, etc. Like collections on account, a sales check or memo should be made out each time such cash is taken in.

The total of daily cash receipts to be accounted for on the daily summary is obtained by adding cash sales, collections on account, and miscellaneous receipts.

The second section, "Cash on Hand," of a daily summary is a count of the cash actually on hand plus the cash that is represented by petty cash slips. The daily summary provides for counts of your total coins, bills, and checks as well as the amount expended for petty cash. The latter is determined by adding the amounts on the individual petty cash slips. By totaling all four of these counts, you obtain the total cash accounted for. To determine the amount of your daily cash deposit, you deduct from the "total cash accounted for" the total of the petty cash and change funds.

Cash to be deposited on the daily summary should always equal the total receipts to be accounted for minus the fixed amount of your petty cash and change funds. If it does not, all the work in preparing the daily summary should be carefully checked. Obviously, an error in giving change, in ringing up a sale, or neglecting to do so, will result in a cash shortage or overage. The daily summary provides spaces for such errors so that the proper entries can be made in your bookkeeping records. The last section of your daily summary, "Sales," records the total daily sales broken down into (1) cash sales and (2) charge sales.

As soon as possible after the daily summary has been completed, all cash for deposit should be taken to the bank. A duplicate deposit slip, stamped by the bank, should be kept with the daily summary as evidence that the deposit was made.

B. Petty Cash and Charge Funds

The record of, daily, sales and cash. Receipts which we have just described. is designed. on the assumption that a petty cash fund and a change cash fund, or a combination change and petty cash fund, are used. All businesses, small and large, have day-to-day expenses that are so small they do not warrant the drawing of a check. Good management practice calls for careful control of such expenses. The petty cash fund provides such control. It is a sum of money which is obtained by drawing a check to provide several days, a week's, or a month's need of cash for small purchases. The type of business will determine the amount of the petty cash fund.

Each time a payment is made from the petty cash, a slip should be made out. If an invoice or receipt is available, it should be attached to the petty- cash slip. The slips and the money ordinarily, but not necessarily, are kept separate from other currency in your cash till, drawer, or register. At all times, the total of unspent petty cash and petty cash slips should equal the fixed amount of the fund. When the total of the slips approaches the fixed amount of the petty cash fund, a check is drawn for the total amount of the slips. The money from this check is used to bring the fund back to its fixed amount.

In addition to a petty cash fund, some businesses that receive cash in over-the-counter transactions have a change fund. The amount needed for making change varies with the size and type of business, and, in some cases, with the days of the week. Control of the money in your change fund will be made-easier, however, if you set a fixed amount large enough to meet all the ordinary change-making needs of your business. Each day, when the day's receipts are balanced and prepared for a bank deposit, you will retain bills and coins totaling the fixed amount of the fund for use the following day. Since you had that amount on hand before you made the day's first sale, the entire amount of the day's receipts will still be available for your bank deposit.

In some cases, the petty cash fund is kept in a petty cash box or safe, apart from the change fund. However, the same fund can serve for both petty cash and change. For example, if you decide that you need $50 for making change and $25 for petty cash, one $75 fund can be used. Whenever, in balancing the day's operations, you see that the petty cash slips total more than $25, you can write a petty cash check for the amount of the slips.

C. Record of Cash Disbursement

To safeguard your cash, it is recommended that all receipts be deposited in a bank account and that all disbursements, except those made from the petty cash fund, are made by drawing a check on that account. Your bank account should be used exclusively for business transactions. If your business is typical, you will have to write checks for merchandise purchases, employee's salaries, rent, utilities, payroll taxes, petty cash, and various other expenses. Your check stubs will serve as a record of cash disbursements.

The checkbook stub should contain all the details of the disbursement including the date, payee, amount and purpose of the payment. In addition, a running balance of the amount you have in your bank account should be maintained by subtracting the amount of each check from the existing balance after the previous check was drawn. If the checks of your checkbook are prenumbered, it is important to mark plainly in the stub when a check is voided for one reason or another.

Each check should have some sort of written document to support it--an invoice, petty-cash voucher, payroll summary and so on. Supporting documents should be approved by you or someone you have authorized before a check is drawn. They should be marked paid and filed after the check is drawn.

Periodically, your bank will send you a statement of your account and return cancelled checks for which money has been withdrawn from your account. It is important that you reconcile your records with those of the bank. This means that the balances in your checkbook and on the bank statement should agree. Uncashed checks must be deducted from your checkbook balance and deposits not recorded on the bank statement must be added to its balance in order to get both balances to agree.

D . Accounts Receivable Records

If you extend credit to your customers, you must keep an accurate account of your credit sales not only in total as you have done on the daily summary but also by the amount that each individual customer owes you. Moreover, you must be systematic about billings and collections. This is important. It results in better relations with your charge customers and in fewer losses from bad debts.

The simplest method of handling accounts receivable--other than just keeping a file of sales-slip carbons--is to have an account sheet for each credit customer. Charge sales and payments on charge sales are posted to each customer sheet. Monthly billing to each of your charge customers should be made from their individual account sheets.

At least two or three times a year, your accounts receivable should be aged. You do this by posting each customer's account and his unpaid charges in columns according to age. These columns are labeled: not due; 1 to 30 days past due; 31 to 60 days past due; 61 to 90 days past due; etc. This analysis will indicate those customers who are not complying with your credit terms.

E . Property Records and Depreciation

In every type of business, it is necessary to purchase property and equipment from time to time. This property usually will last for several years, so it would be unrealistic to show the total amount of the purchase as an expense in any one year. Therefore, when this property is set up in the books as an asset, records must be kept to decrease its value over its life. This decrease is known as depreciation. I have mentioned this before during this talk. The amount of the decrease in value in one year, that is, the depreciation, is charged as an expense for the year.

I am talking about this expense, particularly, because no cash is paid out for it. It is a non-cash, not-out-of-pocket expense. You don't have to hand over actual money at the end of the month.

Records should be kept of this because, otherwise, there is a danger that this expense will be overlooked. Yet it is impossible to figure true profit or loss without considering it. When you deduct the depreciation expense from your firm's income, you reduce your tax liabilities. When you put this depreciation expense into a depreciation allowance account, you are keeping score on your "debt" to depreciation.

In a barber shop, to take a simple example, depreciation of its chairs, dryers, and clippers at the end of the year amounts to $136. You deduct this $136 from the shop's income, in this case, to pay the debt credited to your depreciation allowance account. Since this equipment has the same depreciation value each year, the depreciation allowance account at the end of 3 years will show that a total of $408 worth of equipment has been used up. The books of the barbershop therefore show an expense of $408 which actually has not been spent. It is in the business to replace the depreciated equipment. If replacement will not take place in the immediate future, the money can be used in inventory, or in some other way to generate more sales or profits.

How you handle this money depends on many things. You can set it aside at a low interest rate and have that much less operating money. Or you can put it to work in your business where it will help to keep your finances healthy.

Remember, however, that you must be prepared financially when it is time to buy replacement equipment. A depreciation allowance account on your books can help to keep you aware of this. It helps you keep score on how much depreciation or replacement money you are using in your business.

Keeping score with a depreciation allowance account helps you to know when you need to convert some of your assets into replacement cash. If, for example, you know on January 1 that Your delivery truck will be totally depreciated by June 30, you can review the situation objectively. You can decide whether you ought to use the truck longer or replace it. If you decide to replace it, then you can plan to accumulate the cash, and time the purchase in order to make the best deal.

F. Schedule of Insurance Coverage

The schedule of insurance coverage is prepared to indicate the type of coverage and the amount presently in force. This schedule should list all the insurance carried by your business-- fire and extended coverage, theft, liability, life, business interruption and so forth.

This schedule should be prepared to present the following: name of insurance company, annual premium, expiration date, type of coverage, amount of coverage, asset insured, and estimated current value of asset insured.

An analysis of this schedule should indicate the adequacy of insurance coverage. A review of this schedule with your insurance agent is suggested.

V. CONCLUSION

During the brief time allotted to this subject of the basic fundamentals of bookkeeping, we have just scratched its surface. What we have tried to do is to inform you, as small-business managers, of the importance of good records. We have described the components of the important records that you must have if you are going to manage your business efficiently and profitably. In addition, we have brought to your attention some of the subsidiary records that will aid you in managing your business.

There are other records such as breakeven charts, budgets, cost accounting systems, to mention a few, which can also benefit the progressive manager. However, we do not have the time even to give you the highlights of those management tools. Your accountant can assist you in learning to understand and use them. Moreover, he can help you to develop and use the records we have discussed. For further information about them, you also can read the publications of the Small Business Administration, some of which are available to you free of charge.

By reading and using the accounting advice available to you, you can make sure that you have the right records to improve your managing skill and thereby increase your profits.
